The Way We Were

The Way We Were

Personal Reflections on Life in the Ozarks

A Collection of Articles from the
Howell County News

Lonnie Whitaker

Scrivener Oak Press · St. Louis, Missouri

First Edition: 2023
Published by Scrivener Oak Press
St. Louis, Missouri

Paperback ISBN: 979-8-9857780-8-3
E-book ISBN: 979-8-9857780-9-0
Library of Congress Control Number: 2023911142

Book Design: Peggy Nehmen, n-kcreative.com
Cover background photo by Yinan Chen, Missouri Cuivre River.
https://commons.wikimedia.org/wiki/File:Gfp-missouri-cuivre-river-state-park-lake-view.jpg

Nostalgic cover photos property of Lonnie Whitaker.

CONTENTS

For Mary Ellen

Preface

THE STORIES IN THIS book are from my newspaper column, "The Way We Were . . . Personal Reflections on Life in the Ozarks," published by the Howell County News, a weekly print and online newspaper in Willow Springs, Missouri. More information about the paper is available at howellcountynews.com.

—LONNIE WHITAKER

Acknowledgements

I OWE THANKS TO many people for their contributions to this project and will mention a few.

The teachers, friends, schoolmates, relatives, and Ozark storytellers from Shannon and Howell Counties who provided a wealth of writing material and made growing up in the southern-Missouri Ozarks a blessing.

Any mention of this area of Missouri would be remiss if I didn't thank my friend and former U.S. Congressman, two-term Missouri Treasurer, and four-term Missouri state representative, Wendell Bailey, for his personal assistance and the example he set in his numerous campaigns.

Amanda and Ron Mendez, the owners of the Howell County News, for providing the opportunity for me to share my stories.

Peggy Nehmen, co-owner of Nehmen-Kodner and book designer, for designing a brilliant cover; patiently shepherding this book from concept to distribution; and providing a collaborative experience.

Deborah Schott for her encouragement and helpful input on my writing efforts.

My wife, Mary Ellen, who proofreads each column, and invariably finds mistakes that I miss.

The New Kid in Town

WHEN I FIRST MOVED to Willow Springs in 1959, the summer before the 7th grade, I was the new kid in town from the country. I moved from my grandparents' Shannon County farm and attending a two-room school at Montier, to living with my mother and stepfather in a town with a junior high school.

It seemed to me that I had moved to a metropolis. In actual fact, the city limits sign read "Population 1,913." It remained that way for years, even after the census of 1960. Nevertheless, we had TV reception and indoor plumbing. I hope to elaborate on country cisterns and TV reception in a future article.

But it was easy to make friends in Willow because of organized summer baseball at Booster Field. Playing on an actual ballfield instead of a cow pasture with firewood sticks for bases was a dream.

I still remember many of the boys who suited up that summer. Truman Grogan, our main pitcher had 13 strikeouts in one game, and was awarded a trophy at the end of the season for the best sportsman (I'll wager he still has it.). Others included the Zimmerman twins, a lefty and a righty; Jimmy "Tee" Thomas, who owned a first baseman's mitt, anchored first; Eddie Mack Hill, relief pitcher and third base; Kenny Thompson in the outfield: and Jimmy Kilpatrick.

One day before Coach Arnold Copeland, the owner of the town's only Corvette, arrived for practice, Jimmy and I got into a scuffle. It started as a shoving match but escalated into a fist fight. It ended when I landed a lucky haymaker on Jimmy's nose. We shook hands and never had a cross word afterwards. But if the truth be told, I suspect Jimmy would have won Round 2. When Jimmy died this year in March, I remembered our friendship and the innocence of our altercation.

That summer marked a milestone for Little League baseball in Willow. It was the first year the teams had real uniforms. Local businesses sponsored the gray uniforms, with navy blue lettering. For their generosity, the sponsors advertised their businesses above the number on the back of the jerseys: Padgett's Hardware, Bank of Willow Springs, People's Drugs, Daisy Queen, and others.

At least one business remained anonymous. My stepfather, a Willow businessman, donated to the cause, but the name of his business didn't show up on the back of a jersey. He owned and operated a tavern on South Center Street, in between Gardiner's secondhand store and Randall's Grocery, across from Harold Adam's coin-operated laundromat. It seems the town fathers thought it inappropriate to saddle a kid with "George's Tavern."

George's tavern ownership caused minor social complications for me. When the topic at Sunday school at the First Baptist Church was the evils of alcohol, I cringed as it seemed every eye in class focused on me. Incidentally, the Sunday school teacher was Neil Pamperein, the longtime math and science teacher at WSHS, and later, at Southwest Missouri State–West Plains.

Mr. Pamperein passed away last month, and his memory is a reminder of the blessings alums have received from quality teachers in Willow Springs. Perhaps, an article on teachers is warranted.

Those were the days, my friends. *American Graffiti*, *The Waltons*, or Mayberry all remind of growing up in the Ozarks and my hometown, Willow Springs, population 1,913.

Recollections of School Days

IN A PREVIOUS ARTICLE, I mentioned the blessings received from teachers. This article commemorates the early careers of two storied teachers, whose 40-plus-year careers culminated in the Liberty School system.

It did not seem like a blessing in the winter of 1956 when I transferred from a city school in Davenport, Iowa, to the Montier School, a few miles east of Mtn. View. With its musty smelling books from a past generation, the country schoolhouse built in the 1920s hardly seemed like a setting for effective learning.

It was the end of an era, before the rural school districts consolidated with the town systems. The white clapboard structure, which had one main classroom divided by a heavy wooden folding door, had no indoor plumbing or air-conditioning. The students used outdoor toilets and washed their hands in water drawn from a cistern. Windows and potbelly stoves controlled the temperature.

But in the larger urban schools, full of post-WW II baby boomers, I had easily been lost in the crowd, and was a C student at best. The country school, with smaller classes and attentive teachers, proved to be a turning point in my education—and in my life.

On that first day as a third-grader at Montier, I met Mrs. Margaret Shockley and her husband, Wilbert, who would be my teachers for the next three years. They taught all eight grades, which totaled less than fifty students.

In her mid-twenties, Mrs. Shockley with her fair complexion and auburn red hair, still looked like the girl who had been the prettiest in her high school class. Her attractive face belied the sternness that could cloud up at the hint of a lie. One boy I recall learned that lesson the hard way, and through the seat of his pants, in an incident involving a "controlled" substance—chewing tobacco.

Mr. Shockley, a star high school baseball player, had dropped out his senior year to join the fighting in the south Pacific. His love of athletics generated vigorous softball games at recess and noon that taught lessons about fairness and equality.

In these games, gender-equity was the norm. Fielding two teams required boys, girls, and teachers. In choosing teams, boys learned to pick the best players regardless of sex, and it often wasn't "boys first." The Shockleys would usually play with the weaker team.

After Mr. Shockley cried, "Play ball," it was just one team against the other. But when one team left the field to bat, it was also the norm to leave ball gloves in field for those who didn't own one.

Managing four grades in each room required innovative teaching techniques. The Shockleys gave assignments and later summoned each class to the "recitation bench." Today, these are known as breakout sessions. Older students helped the younger ones. Today, this is known as mentoring. Advanced students could audit the class next to them for accelerated learning. Today, we plan programs for the gifted.

Mr. and Mrs. Shockley were proud when their students transferred to high schools that they were generally ahead of the town students.

I remember what a treat it was when Mr. Shockley read from a classic book such as Tom Sawyer. A natural actor, his tone and inflection changed to create the voices of Tom, Huck, or Aunt Polly. The room was otherwise silent. His reading had a subtle teaching angle, too. It put all four grades on the same level.

One incident underscored the benevolence behind their teaching abilities. Mrs. Shockley noticed a student wearing worn-out shoes with flapping soles and exposed toes. Conscious of the boy's pride, Mr. and Mrs. Shockley conspired to get him new shoes without causing embarrassment.

They recruited me into their plan. I sat with the boy, ostensibly to study spelling, but actually to compare my shoes to his to determine the right size. "Your foot's bigger than mine." "No, it isn't." "Well, let's see."

The ruse worked, and during recess a few days later, the Shockleys presented the boy with a pair of sturdy new shoes. He beamed, and looked at me and said, "That's why you wanted to compare shoes."

Blessings are often not appreciated at the time they occur. This was different. That day, I knew I was part of something special.

Another incident stands out in my memory. Referring to a grade she had given me, Mrs. Shockley simply said, "You can do better than that." Something about the way she said it made me believe her. I suspect I am not the only one who took her words to heart.

A decade ago I visited Mrs. Shockley, and she reminded me how different it was back then. "Once, I had to excuse a boy from the eighth grade so he could register for the draft," she said. Although it was unusual to have an 18-year-old eighth grader, it was not odd to have students repeat grades because they missed class to work on the family farm.

Teacher Margaret Shockley with her 4th grade student
Lonnie Whitaker in front of the Montier Grocery in May 1957,
the night of his brother Jack's eighth grade graduation.

The school was consolidated a few years after I began, but the Shockleys continued to teach for many years. Today, the schoolhouse in Montier no longer stands, and Mr. Shockley and Mrs. Shockley are deceased.

The Shockleys were never able to have children of their own after Mrs. Shockley lost twins prematurely, but the couple's legacy as encouraging, caring teachers continues today in the lives of the children they taught.

One former student is none other than former Missouri Governor Bob Holden. Others are doctors, lawyers, farmers, moms, dads, and, not surprisingly, teachers. And, all were enlightened by these two heroes.

Lonnie Whitaker in front of the Montier School circa 1968.

When Fall Comes to the Ozarks

WHEN FALL COMES TO the Ozarks, besides the beauty of the turning leaves, two things come to mind: football and the Fall Fiesta. My first experience with both happened in Willow Springs in 1959.

That year marked the first year Willow Springs had a junior high football team. The Willow Cubs, coached by Charles "Buddy" Bennett, fielded a team of 19 7th and 8th graders in spanking new uniforms.

We played West Plains and Mtn. View twice each and lost all four games. But our enthusiasm was not quelled. After all, we got to use the same locker room as the high schoolers, play on Palenske Field, ride a bus to away games, and we had cheerleaders.

Our cheerleaders didn't lose their enthusiasm either. I remember them practicing in Carol (Hale) Aldridge's yard and one of their cheers: "Can you make it? Can you make it? Can you Alabama–shake it?" Where in the world did they get that cheer? Carol remembers the cheer but not the origin.

Consulting with schoolmates, I learned that recollections of who made up the 7th grade cheer squad are sketchy, and who the 8th grade cheerleaders were, even sketchier. But for the next year, 1960, I can identify the cheerleaders with certainty. That year some of the country schools such as Noblett consolidated with Willow, and it was the year the *Willamizzou* staff produced a grade school yearbook, the *Willomizzette*.

A photograph in the *Willomizzette* shows the 8th grade cheer-leaders: Jenny Mae Bolerjack, Sandy Flake, Carol Hale, Peggy Henry, Sandy Merrill, Sherry Pruett, and Annette Tetrick. And from the 7th grade: Mary Hanks, Cathy Clift, Jackie Patton, Carolyn Sherrill, and Sandra Gilmore.

The Cubs took great pride battling against our arch rival, West Plains. Every Willow boy learned from an early age that the Zizzers were the enemy, and too often, a nemesis of the Bears. But back then, West Plains junior high teams were not called the Zizzers. They went by the nickname Whizzers. They are no longer called that. I suspect that a latter-day connotation of the word compelled a change of name.

Before any player could suit up, permission had to be obtained from a parent. All the wannabe players were sent home with a mimeographed form to be signed.

Ivy Grogan did not want her son Truman playing football. Basketball was OK, but not football. She refused to sign the form. Now, forgery is a strong word, but Truman presented a permission slip to Coach Bennett, ostensibly signed by his mother. Mrs. Grogan, being a basketball and not a football fan, didn't attend any of the games.

Truman's scheme worked fine until the second game of the next season, when someone ratted him out to his mom. Truman says, "I guess she figured it was too late to complain, because she never said another word about not playing football."

Without controversy, before every kickoff, Coach Bennett huddled the players for a team prayer. I still remember the words. "Lord, help us to win, and if we should win, help us to be good winners. But if we should lose, help us to be good losers." When he finished the prayer, his reverent tone changed to a battle cry: "Now, go out there and get those rascals." Eddie Mack Hill, who was our quarterback, used to say that Coach Bennett used a stronger noun than "rascals."

Moving from the playground to the gridiron, required new skills. We learned the basic X's and O's of the game, blocking, and tackling, but our special team skills, such as punting, took longer to master.

Bill Tandy, an eighth-grader on the team, says, "I recall running toward the punt receiver and hearing a loud thud on top of my helmet making my ears ring [and] the football bounced off my head right in front of me. I ended up in a pile of players scrambling to recover the ball. The referee broke up the dogpile and stated the ball was down where it hit the Willow player, and he pointed at me."

In addition to coaching junior high sports and high school baseball, Mr. Bennett taught high school biology and 8th grade health. Much of his health class focused on human anatomy. We had to memorize the major muscles and bones of the body.

In my view, he was an excellent teacher, but to the chagrin of some, he would use class time on game days to diagram football and basketball plays on the blackboard. But his straightforward approach in teaching made retention of the information easier. Perhaps that's why I still remember the wrist has eight bones.

Mr. Bennett told me only two students had ever scored a perfect 400 points in a semester in his classes—me and a high school student who I understand became a nurse. No doubt she used the information from his biology class, while I'm still waiting for "eight bones in the wrist" to come up as the answer in a trivia contest.

In the second season, the Cub's record improved to 2-1-1, beating Mtn. View 33 to 0 and West Plains 29 to 21. We tied Ava and lost to Mtn. Grove.

Six players from that 8th grade class, Terry Collins, Jody Corn, Truman Grogan, Jimmy Johnson, Lonnie Whitaker, and Danny Zimmerman, four years later, in 1964, started on the varsity football team that came within 6 points of winning an SCA championship. Our consolation prize was beating the Zizzers that year.

I will highlight the Fall Fiesta in a future article.

Beauty Shops In Willow

WHEN I COMMENT ON a woman's new haircut, the response is often one of surprise. I tell them I was raised in a beauty shop. Well, not actually, but I did spend considerable time in ones owned by my mother, Opal Rothwell.

When I was in high school, my mother, who always had a knack for cutting hair, decided to become a licensed beautician. She started her quest working as an apprentice for Thelma Haycraft at the Cut & Curl Salon on Main Street across from Dr. Amos Coffee's office.

Incidentally, Thelma was Charles, Buddy, Mike, and Pat Stuart's grandmother. In my first novel, *Geese to a Poor Market*, Buddy noticed I named a fictional beauty shop the Cut & Curl as an homage to that shop.

The problem with apprenticing is it takes about twice as long to get a beauty license as going to beauty school—over two years compared to less than a year. So my mother decided to enroll at the Blue Bonnet Beauty School in Springfield, MO.

Since I was a junior at WSHS, she arranged for me to board at Truman Grogan's home.

Paul Faulkenberry, one of the instructors at Blue Bonnet, had graduated from Southwest Missouri State as a theater major before becoming a beauty instructor. Using his theatrical talents, Paul directed the students at Blue Bonnet in the play, *Cinderella*. Paul cast himself as Prince Charming and arranged for the production to be carried on KYTV. My mother had a minor role and insisted that I come to Springfield to see the play.

When I arrived on set before the TV tape started rolling, Mom introduced me to Paul. With stage makeup, purple tights, and teased, bouffant platinum hair, Paul was an avant-garde sight to behold for a teenage country boy. I would learn years later that Paul was a remarkably talented man.

Fast forward fifty years to around 1990, when my wife and I were dating. We were having lunch when she said had to go to "Paul" for a haircut. I had a flashback. "You don't by chance mean Paul Faulkenberry?" She looked surprised and wanted to know how I knew Paul. "It's a long story," I said.

It turns out that after Blue Bonnet, Paul had quite a career. He sang with the Dallas Opera, auditioned for the Paris Opera, became a top hairstylist in St. Louis, and in the nineties owned an antique store, with a beauty shop in the back. [Here's a personal aside. Schoolmate Sadie Burns and I used to kid my mother that we were going to open a shop called "Sadie and Lon's Salon—with Saloon in back."]

After Paul's store was burglarized several times, he decided it was time to move back home to Shannon County. He acquired his parents' Victorian-style house in Eminence, furnished it with inventory from his antiques store, and opened a bed and breakfast. And, of course, he started directing city-wide plays.

My wife and I stayed several times at his B&B and watched rehearsals for entertainment or listened to Paul read poetry in the parlor. I told him I could never write poetry. He said, in his dramatic, baritone voice, "Oh, you probably could."

You, gentle reader, be the judge.

Paul's Celebrity Ball

An interesting fellow, this friend of mine, Paul.

The first time we met he hardly notice at all, when he was

In charge of the Celebrity Ball.

All the rich women, the big and the small,

Had to have Paul or no one at all

To perform magic creations, bouffant, not banal.

Like twittering birds this gaggle of girls

As Paul twisted and stretched and worked on their curls.

But what of his regulars—his special pet hens?

The shop was so full they couldn't get in.

Militant blue-hairs and angry old grays said

Let us in, Paul, or you'll long rue this day.

We'll march in the streets and we'll cluck and
    we'll quack.

It's you who'll be sorry, we'll never come back.

On Donner on Prancer, no that's not my line

I don't know what's worse, prom week or Christmas time.

Day into night, no matter how long,

Paul stepped to the door and said, "The show must
    go on!"

Back to his scissors, he was quick on his feet
Until all the actors' hair was complete.
Then came the show and Paul, tails, tux and all
Sat down at the piano to play for the ball.
The selection was imposing, they'd accept nothing less
From the one they had picked to play next to closing.

After beauty school, Mom had several shops in Willow. I started getting my hair cut there, after I no longer wore a flattop, she gave a better haircut that the local barbers. My apologies to Red, Gene, Boob, and Mr. Barnes.

I have interesting memories from her shops. One teetotalling, church-going lady, ironically, liked getting her set with beer. Beer is a pretty good setting lotion. After it dries, it combs out nicely and doesn't weigh the hair down. My mother always cautioned the lady not to go to church on a rainy day, or she could expect a visit from the preacher on Monday morning.

While I didn't have a second thought about cruising into her shops, it made some of her patrons uncomfortable—like the day I saw Mrs. Munford in brush rollers. For those who don't remember her, she taught English at WSHS for forty years and was our Jennifer Jones in *Good Morning, Miss Dove*. She had an implied highhandedness that could put a smart aleck in his place by raising a eyebrow. Always impeccably dressed from stores in Springfield, her hair was never out of place. And that day when I saw her in rollers . . . she didn't flinch. But I was as embarrassed as if I had seen her in her nightgown.

My mother never had a daughter, but she truly loved the girls she worked with, and I would be remiss if I didn't mention some of them: Brenda (Brown) Thompson, Peggy (Henry) Bradford, Janice (Corn James), and Nita Ray.

On a personal note, I want to thank everyone for the thoughtful comments I have received about my articles.

7TH Grade Remembered

THE HEADLINE IN THE 1960 *Willamizzou* announced: "7th grade: largest in history." We had 59 students and two teachers, Mrs. Madden and Mrs. Cape. Our classrooms were on the second floor of the old school building built in 1894, which was demolished a few years later to make room for the new high school, which is now 55-years-old. Our class was the first to graduate from it.

Dorothy Cape taught most of us. Serious and firm, but she would laugh if something struck her as humorous. I think it helped that she had raised two boys of her own before she encountered the yahoos in my class. Like on the day we were supposed to give oral presentations.

My best buddy Truman Grogan and I decided to perform our version of the Bull of the Woods Chewing Tobacco commercial that was on TV at the time. In the TV commercial, a young bull wanted to sing in the Bull of the Woods Quartet, but his voice was too high-pitched, and he was being coached by an older bull. Truman played the part of the young bull, and I played the part of the older coach.

During our presentation Truman sang in a squeaky falsetto, and I strained my vocal cords striving for a deep, mellifluous voice. After I crooned the catchphrase "flavored with fruit," instead of repeating it, Truman squeaked, "Rooty, toot, toot." The class thought it was hilarious, and even Mrs. Cape cracked a smile, although I suspect she had hoped for something a bit more educational.

Mary Pierce, always a good student, supplied a less theatrical effort, but signed off her presentation with the initials G.E, which she said stood for Girl Einstein. Another smile from Mrs. Cape.

Mrs. Cape's Christian patience, however, could be tried. One of my sources reminded me that she applied some discipline to the bottom of a couple miscreants who wouldn't quit rough-housing during recess.

For an art lesson one day, Mrs. Cape stacked a tubular-shaped tennis ball cannister on top of a cigar box and told us to draw it. Until that day, I harbored the idea that I had some artistic ability. I could draw the profile of Micky Mouse's head. But Ricard Smith's rendition of the assignment disavowed me of that notion and blew away the competition.

Richard captured the three-dimensional aspects in perfect proportion, with shading and texture, including the writing and artwork on the cigar box. It's not surprising, a few years later, Richard scored high on a portion of the Differential Aptitude Test we took as juniors. I'm sure I didn't.

I sat across from Sherry Pruett. I remember because she had a cool transistor radio. Remember those? But she had the coolest—a red Magnavox—that could pick up more stations than just KUKU. I coveted one in the display case of Sol and Lola Coker's TV repair shop on North Maple, between Main and Third Streets.

But apparently it wasn't only the radio I admired. Notes in my *Willamizzou* that year from Carol Hale and Jenny Mae Bolerjack wished me luck in the future with Sherry. Hmmm?

Because of alphabetical seating, I sat near the Zimmerman twins, Danny and David. Identical and hard to tell apart, they often made their presence known. Danny once commented about his mother's recent pregnancy that caused one girl to say he shouldn't be talking such matters in class.

A classmate told me if I ever got into a fight with one of the Zimmerman twins, to watch out because the other one would jump you. Maybe so, but I never had a cross word with either of them.

Incidentally, the Zimmermans' parents owned the *Willow Springs News*, and David and Danny had their own byline, "Our Tickle Column," which featured one-line jokes and riddles.

Now, a sad note. Earlier this fall David passed away, and my thoughts have been with Danny, who is recovering from a bad fall.

The spring of 1960 was the first year for junior high track and field. As soon as basketball season was over, Coach Bennett issued the thinclad hopefuls sweatpants and hooded sweatshirts and started us running on the streets around the school, until the track at Palenske Field dried out. The winter of 1959-60 was particularly snowy and required makeup days that kept us in school until nearly June.

Running, at least fast running, required ability I did not possess. To the extent I had any talent, it would be on the field part of track and field. Nevertheless, Coach Bennett required everybody to participate in at least one running event at the track meets. The slowest of the plodders were relegated to the mile run—four times around the track—which brings back yet another memory of personal failure.

Winning a medal in the mile run was never a possibility for me. My challenge was not coming in last, and the only person between me and that disgrace was an eighth grader—Bill Tandy. At each track meet, Bill and I raced for the distinction of being next-to-last. I am sad to report that Bill always won that honor. But few years ago, I went out to Palenske Field to see if I could still run a mile—and I could. I think I can take Tandy, now.

Cruising and the A&W

PERHAPS THE FAVORITE TEENAGE pastime in the 1960s was cruising. The Beach Boys based a musical career on cruising and surfing. In Willow Springs we didn't have a surf, but we made an artform out of cruising.

In Willow the "main drag," was Main Street (Highway 60), from the "Little Y" to the Daisy Queen, aka the DQ, owned by Joe and Thelma Baker. The Bakers also owned the adjacent U–Save gas station, which had handy public restrooms. Other stations had restrooms, but the U–Save provided a discreet, drive–up rear entry for a pitstop.

For pilgrims and tourists, the spatial relations may require some explanation. The Little Y was the split between Highway 60 and Springfield Road on the north end of town, just past the present City Hall and the stately Charles Ferguson house. The paved area between the two streets provided an easy turnaround or a temporary parking spot. The "Big Y" was a couple miles southeast of town, where Highway 63 veered south toward West Plains, and Highway 60 continued eastward toward Mtn. View.

Friday and Saturday nights were cruising nights. Whether you had a date or not, it was important to be out and about, to see who else was out and about. Remember, texting and email did not exist.

In the fashion of the era, girls on dates sat in the middle of the front bench seats snuggled next to their guy, who typically had one hand draped over the steering wheel and the other around his girl. Local highway patrolman Lem Carter claimed to have stopped one fellow to suggest that he use two hands. The driver reportedly replied that he needed to use one hand to drive.

Parents would ask what you did all night. A typical response: "We went to the movie." As the cross examination continued, and it had been established that the movie only lasted two hours, they wanted an accounting for the rest of the time. "Oh, nothing. Just dragging Main." "For two hours?"

After finding the gas tank nearly empty the next morning, some parents grew suspicious, and started checking the odometer. "Where did you really go last night? You put 50 miles on the car."

Parents didn't understand that the roundtrip, from the Little Y to the DQ was about 5 miles, which could easily be completed 6- or 7-times in a night. Throw in a side-trip out Pine Grove Road to the roller rink; a sojourn to climb the Blue Buck fire tower; or an expedition to Cabool to check things out, and voila, it's 50 miles.

Not to be outsmarted, some savvy/ornery teenagers learned how to unhook the speedometer cable, which kept the odometer from computing mileage. This created other issues. After months of this trickery, deceived parents would end up at Welsh's or

Bacon's tire shops complaining about how quickly their tires had worn out.

Heading east on the Main Drag from the Little Y, the A&W drive-in was a de rigueur stop or pass-through, depending on whether you were hungry or just ogling. Originally owned and operated by Lyle and Maxine James, it provided jobs for high schoolers as carhops.

One former A&W employee, Barbara Sherrill Pigg, who started working there before she was old enough to drive, said, "Lyle taught us great work ethics. He told us the customer is always right. If they get upset, you go to the bathroom and kick the cement wall and come back with a smile on your faces, because in small towns word travels fast, and if you offend a customer the word will get out and people will no longer come back and the business will suffer and we could lose our jobs."

Barbara added, "He and Maxine were special people and were members of the WSHS 1942 class along with my Mom."

I have fond memories of A&W food: Ice cold root beer in glass mugs, Mama and Papa Burgers, fries, milkshakes, and my grandmother's favorite: broasted chicken—pressure-fired and delicious, before I'd ever heard of Colonel Harland Sanders.

In addition to the drive-in, the A&W had a sit-down dining room where you could actually get a steak. I know this for a fact because Neil Hanks bought me one after I made a couple hard tackles on a Thayer tailback. It had to be thawed, and was still bluish and cold in the middle, but I ate it with the gusto and pride of a conquering warrior.

For some, the real draw was the carhops. With help from some A&W alums, here's a partial list: Barbara Sherrill Pigg, Marilyn Sherrill Cummins, Linda Pruett White, Brenda Burns,

Beth Chapin, Deanna Gentry Casebeer, and Sandra Davidson, now an attorney and professor, who recently told me, "I really enjoyed that job."

And there's another carhop I remember well—me. Yes, I was the first (and perhaps only) boy carhop at the A&W, but certainly not why anybody stopped, unless it was some of my buddies to point fingers and razz me—but the novelty soon wore off.

My A&W career started one Saturday, after the A&W was acquired by Raymond and Eula Turner. While eating inside at the restaurant, I overheard Mrs. Turner say one her carhops couldn't show up for work. The concern was evident on her face, as the bays were filling up with cars.

With no hesitation, I volunteered to work for her that night. Her expression turned to surprise, no doubt, because I was a boy, and one who played on all the sports teams. Out of desperation, I suppose, she handed me an apron and put me to work. At the end of the shift she asked if I wanted a job, and I accepted.

My tenure wasn't without a few mishaps along the way. Once, I delivered burgers and two strawberry milkshakes to a man and his wife. I hung the serving tray on his open car door—a rookie mistake. When he closed the door, the two milkshakes landed in his lap. It looked as if he was covered in pink Pepto-Bismol.

Working there was great fun and safer than circling it in my car. One afternoon I was cruising solo around the A&W and stopped for a root beer and to chat with Marilyn Sherrill.

As I drove away, I was apparently paying more attention to Marilyn than my driving, and high-centered my parents' 1962 Ford Galaxy on the highway curb and was stuck.

Embarrassed, I trudged over to Chet Chamberlain's Ford dealership, and Frank David Hicks drove me back in the wrecker and lifted the car off the curb. I don't think Chamberlain every sent a bill, because my mother never mentioned the incident. Now, that's small-town kindness. Or as the Beach Boys might say, small town "good vibrations."

When TV Came to Montier

MOVING FROM A SHANNON County farm to Willow Springs in 1959 meant I could watch TV. Television reception in Montier (7 miles east of Mountain View) in the 1950s was essentially non–existent. In fact, TVs were scarcer than hens' teeth, and in our neck of the woods, there weren't any until my grandparents introduced one to the area.

When my grandparents, Riley and Beulah Casey, lived in the Quad Cities of Iowa and Illinois in the early 1950s, they bought a television. The call of the Ozarks brought them back home to Montier, and they brought the set with them. And there it sat, in the living room of the Shannon County farmhouse, as an altar for photographs of bearded relatives of past generations displayed on it.

It was otherwise useless. Never mind the Ozark Mountains, the nearest television stations were in Memphis, Tennessee, and Springfield, Missouri. Both cities were well outside the range of "rabbit ears," and there were no satellites in the sky. Sputnik, which would later be blamed for cows going dry and hens not laying, would not be launched until 1957.

Riley and Beulah Casey, circa 1956, in front of their farmhouse in Shannon County, Missouri, where Riley erected a 30-foot TV antenna pole to get distant reception.

Riley Casey had a knack for figuring out how to handle practical chores. In part it was born of necessity—he was a one-armed blacksmith. Driving nails was just one example. With his one hand, in a motion like an orchestra conductor wielding a baton, he could pull a nail out of his nail apron, brace it with two fingers against the wooden handle of a claw hammer, draw back, and sink it a quarter-inch in a board, so it was teed up and ready to pound.

Actually, having one hand and a hook sometimes was the necessary mother of invention. But he was no Rube Goldberg, the engineer/cartoonist famous for drawing complicated machines to

solve simple problems. Grandpa's approach was just the opposite: he had simple solutions to complex problems. With a little
hillbilly ingenuity and engineering, Grandpa was going to bring
TV to the Ozarks.

He figured that a tall antenna would be needed to get long-
range reception. At first, he considered putting an antenna on
top of the two-story house, but realized that plan had problems.
Memphis and Springfield were in two different directions; that
would mean climbing on the roof, mostly at night, to turn the
antenna each time they wanted to change stations.

An idea came to him, and he sat at the kitchen table with
my grandmother and drew his plan on a paper napkin. Grandma
approved.

The process started when grandpa went into the woods with
his double-bit ax, cut down a tall white oak tree, trimmed the
limbs, and peeled the bark. The result was a thirty-foot log as
smooth and straight as a telephone pole.

He harnessed our reliable old mare, Dolly, and used her to
drag the pole back to the house.

My brother Jack and I were curious when he salvaged a
three-foot section of stovepipe from the smokehouse. We soon
learned it was to be used as a form in the center of a square
concrete footing. When the cement was poured around the stovepipe, a hole the circumference of the pole was left in the center.

On a Friday night in May 1954, neighbors were invited for
homemade ice cream and cake in celebration of my birthday.
The men were invited back the next morning to help grandpa
with his pole. The leftover cake and fresh coffee would have been

enough to get the men back, but there was the added incentive of seeing a working television.

When the men, Johnny, Mose, and Rocky, all wearing bib overalls, arrived the next morning, Riley led them to the project site. Jack and I tagged along to watch.

The sight of the pole triggered some exaggerated grunting and complaining from the men. "Riley, think you got enough pole here?" Or, "Riley, we need a 'skyhook' for this." Each joshing comment mandated a certain responsive laughter.

Riley and Mose nailed the aluminum antennae to one end of the pole. Then, all together, the men lifted the pole, maneuvered the other end over the stovepipe hole, and began walking it upright like ancient Egyptians setting an obelisk. When the pole was vertical, it slipped perfectly into the hole.

This was to be a directional antenna, and Riley was ready with the final piece. With two tenpenny nails, he attached a thirty-inch two-by-four to the pole about head high. It looked like the handles on a submarine periscope, and was just outside the living room window next to the television.

After connecting the wires to the set, grandpa leaned out the window, and demonstrated how turning the pole with the two-by-four would rotate the aerial.

I still have a vivid picture in my mind of watching television at the old place. Grandpa leaning out the window with Grandma manning the TV controls.

"Ma, you got any picture yet?"

"No, not yet. Keep on turning it, Riley, but just a smidgen."

How was the reception? Intermittent and weather dependent. But at night sitting in front of a snowy screen, it could keep us mesmerized, hoping to see a program all the way through, or to catch a glimpse of a celebrity.

How could I have known back then that the excitement of having the only TV around would, years later, still provide pleasure, as one of my Ozark memories.

Creativity and the Fall Fiesta

ALTHOUGH NO LONGER A part of Willow Springs school culture, the Fall Fiesta was a highlight of the fall semester during my junior high and high school years.

The Fall Fiesta, which started circa 1926, was a school-wide event that involved all grades—elementary, junior high, and high school—and, really, the town as well. King and queen candidates selected from each grade would ride down Main Street, crowded with spectators, on gayly decorated floats.

My first experience with the Fall Fiesta, like many of my first Willow experiences, occurred in 1959. My seventh-grade class selected Phyliss Lovan and me as the queen and king candidates. Two things standout in my memory: Phyliss, a popular girl, was taller than I by several inches, and my mother reluctantly joined the seventh-grade mothers' committee.

Phyliss's height seem to be of more interest to everyone else than it was to me. I was just enamored by the whole event. The Fall Fiesta theme that year was "Wonders of the World." My mother's Ozark upbringing led her to suggest to the committee that the parade float should reflect something they knew about. After all, did anyone know the Colossus of Rhodes? She suggested the Wonder of the Ozarks.

Apparently, the other mothers had nothing better. I have a vague memory of sitting in the middle of cut brush on a flat-bed hay trailer. Our float didn't win any prizes, and Phillis and I weren't crowned, but we are forever commemorated in the 1960 *Willamizzou*. Now, as I think about it, my stepfather's moonshine still would have been a nice addition to the float.

Coronation of the winners happened with great fanfare at an evening talent show that packed the school auditorium. Winners were determined by a point system based on student voting, winning the float competition, and money raised. Classes got a point for each penny raised at bake sales, car washes, leaf raking, or any number of odd jobs.

Being the largest class helped the Class of '65 in school competitions, but it wasn't just our size—we were creative. But sometimes our creativity led to problems.

Our junior year, Pat Montgomery and Jimmy Johnson were our king and queen candidates, and I was the class manager—the designated organizer of float construction and money raising.

The theme that year was movies, and the floats were to reflect the theme. Someone in our class—maybe me—got the not-so-bright idea to base our float on *Premature Burial*, a 1962 horror movie starring Ray Milland, which had been at the Star Theater.

Obviously, we needed a coffin. Classmate Joy Herman's father, a carpenter, agreed to construct one for us. With it, our float was a doozy. Pat, dressed in mourning black of a grieving widow, kneeled next to the black coffin. "Parson" Johnny Jones, with Bible in hand, intoned over Jimmy lying in the coffin. Jimmy, whose face was covered with white, "pancake" makeup, kept rearing up from the coffin to wave at the onlookers along the parade route.

Say it ain't so—our float came in last place. The judges said it was morbid. Other classes, particularly the seniors, who won with a Ben-Hur float, laughed and razzed us.

Losing was new territory for us. The year before, our Roaring 20's float, which won first place, depicted a speakeasy with Queen Glenda Turner as a flapper and King Truman Grogan tending bar. The float was followed by "gangsters" in wheelman Richard Hedrick's Model A Ford, with Jimmy Johnson riding the running board wielding a Tommy gun, and "wounded" Richard Smith draped over the hood.

The sophomore class's Roaring 20s float in the 1963 Fall Fiesta parade, held annually in Willow Springs, Missouri.

In spite of the faux pas with our coffin float, it turned out that our detractors had buried us prematurely. Because we had raised so much money, our class still won the overall competition and crowned Pat and Jimmy.

But one of our creative money-raising schemes backfired, bigtime. One Saturday afternoon, the class had set up a bake sale table in front of Ferguson's drugs, owned by Sadie Ruth and Tommy Ferguson. Some customers gave us money and told us to keep the baked goods, and it occurred to a couple "geniuses" at the scene, who will remain anonymous, that soliciting donations would be would be a clever idea.

The two boys crossed the street to Pagett's Hardware and bought a tin cup to enhance their promotion and headed to People's Drugs, owned by Frank Protiva, looking for donors. It isn't clear whether they found any benefactors there, but they did find a business card lying on the counter. And it changed everything. The printing on the card showed hand-shaped symbols of the American Sign Language alphabet used by the hearing impaired.

They taped the card on the tin cup, and began collecting money as street performers acting the roles of a hearing-impaired person and his interpreter. Everything seemed ducky until the real hearing-impaired man put money in their cup. A man the boys had never seen before.

The boys tried to give him the money back, but he refused and pointed at the card on the cup, as if he thought the boys were deaf, too. They tried to explain that they could hear just fine, but had little success, because the man couldn't hear them, and they didn't understand sign language. Embarrassed and dripping with guilt, they removed the card from the cup and gave the man all the money they had collected.

At the time, it was it was just another teenage stunt gone awry, with no thought of harm. Now, of course, it would be rightly viewed with recrimination. Even back then, I suspect if the boys had simply put two and two together, they would have been less creative. But I would have one less story to tell.

Tip a Canoe and Tyler, Too

I **LEARNED TO SWIM** in Jacks Fork (more about my favorite creek in a future story), but I took my first lifesaving lessons in Smokey Stover's "indoor" pool in Willow Springs.

Smokey owned a motel on Main Street located approximately where the Sonic is today, and built the pool adjacent to it in the early 1960s.

To describe it as an indoor pool is a bit of a stretch. In actual fact, it was an outdoor pool housed inside aqua-and yellow-colored, corrugated fiberglass walls and a roof. It was heated and open year-round. Nevertheless, he claimed it was the only indoor pool between Springfield and Memphis.

The concept was viewed with some suspicion by adults but welcomed by the kids, because at that time, the nearest swimming pool was in Cabool.

Willow hadn't had a swimming pool in years. An empty, defunct one, which Lyle James had lifeguarded at as a teen, lay empty and weed-filled north of town.

But Smokey's pool is where I obtained Red Cross Lifesaving badges, which gave me the prerequisites for a Red Cross Water Safety Instructor Certification (WSI).

In the summer of 1966, with my newly acquired WSI, I was hired as the waterfront director for Camp Clover Point, a 4-H camp on the Lake of the Ozarks.

Located near Kaiser, Missouri, on a small cove of the lake five miles south of the Grand Glaze Bridge, the former Civilian Conservation Corps camp had provided a rustic camping experience for mid-Missouri 4-H'ers since the late forties.

On my arrival, the camp director asked, "What do you know about canoes?" I elaborated on my experience floating the Jacks Fork, and added that I could "gunwale jump" (a foolish trick to propel a canoe forward by standing upright on the rear gunwales and pumping one's legs up and down). "Good, you're in charge of canoe instruction," he said, and gave me a book. "It explains the 'J-stroke'." I had never heard of the J-stroke.

The waterfront of the camp consisted of a square floating dock for lake swimming in a roped off area, and a grassy shoal where the canoes were stored and launched. The campers (after instruction) could paddle in the three-acre cove.

The first week, two pre-teen paddlers became damsels in distress when they swamped their canoe about forty yards out. Of course, they had on life jackets, and the air pockets on either end of the canoe kept it from sinking to the bottom, but their cries for help were earnest and loud.

I might as well have been singing Mighty Mouse's line "Here I come to save the day . . ." given the heroic charge I made to my canoe. Twenty yards into the rescue I swamped the rescue canoe. From the dock, I heard a chorus of laughter and hooting, which was mostly from my two lifeguard colleagues, but even the two victims started laughing.

With some corrective action, I got the two girls and their canoe back to shore, but it was without glory. Had I bothered to read the instruction book the director had given me, I might have learned that with one person, a canoe is more stable if such person is in the center and not the back of the canoe.

The infamy of the botched rescue did not stop that day. Camp procedure dictated that campers should not call staff members by their first names, or formally, by "Mr." or "Miss." Each year, a "name the staff" contest was held to give each staffer a nickname that campers would use.

Some budding historian remembered the campaign slogan from the presidential election of 1840: "Tippecanoe and Tyler, too." I became "Tippy" for the rest of the summer. Dale, the other male lifeguard, became "Ty." The female lifeguard, Cindi, became "Tweet," because she blew her whistle a lot.

My ego would have preferred "Curly" (even though my hair was straight), or, perhaps, "Geronimo," or "Tarzan," but I was Tippy. I suppose I should have been grateful they didn't nickname me "Tipsy."

Cat Fishing with Felix

AS MENTIONED IN PREVIOUS articles, in the 1950s my brother Jack, the longtime CEO of the Willow Care complex of enterprises, and I lived with our grandparents on a farm in Shannon County.

During the winter of 1958, Jack was diagnosed (perhaps misdiagnosed) with some non-specific illness, and missed classes for several weeks during his freshman year of high school.

In retrospect, given his symptoms—fatigue, low-grade fever, and sore throat—I suspect he had mononucleosis. However, since I have a J.D. and not an M.D., I will stipulate my suspicion is a matter of speculation and inadmissible.

On the other hand, as a "word tinkerer," I claim some latitude. And in this case, according to my grandfather, the doctor told him Jack may have just grown too fast. I rest my case.

Nevertheless, Jack stayed home from school at the Shannon County farmhouse. He spent much of his time in a rocking chair near the wood-burning stove playing with Felix, a solid white, fourteen-pound tomcat.

Felix, in one of his previous nine lives, possibly could have been a union organizer or a hitman. He could be a schmoozer or an enforcer, a mouser or a lap kitty, as circumstances required.

His charm and versatility earned him indoor privileges, which was unusual for a farm cat. He had the best of both worlds: he could roam the fields hunting or come inside and curl up by the stove.

Jack developed a game with Felix he called "cat fishing." The rules of the game were simple and nobody kept score, but a game could last for several minutes, until Felix got tired. The only equipment was a fiberglass fishing rod and a Johnson Century spinning reel.

Jack attached a small cork ball (bobber) to the nearly-invisible, monofilament line of his pole and repeatedly cast the ball across the living room over Felix's head. Felix would leap vertically well over a foot and snatch the ball in mid-air.

Day after day, Jack and Felix played this game. Felix seemed to enjoy the competition, and with the continued practice, became quite proficient.

This athletic prowess translated into misfortune for our grandmother's parakeet, Tweety. One day, when Grandma was cleaning the cage, her precious bird flew from the cage and sported around the living room in frantic flight from one make-shift perch to another.

Tweety's movements were not unnoticed by Felix. Imagine this image with me. Felix's feline senses on full-alert status. His eyes locked on the aerial activity, shifting quickly, and synchronized with the every move the bird made. Crouched and ready to pounce, the muscles in his front paws alternately tensed and relaxed like a tennis player waiting on service.

Felix's tail began to flick from side-to-side. Intuitive calculations provided by nature precisely measured the time and distance coefficients of this avian vector. His timing was perfect. He caught the target swooping too low at two o'clock high, about three feet from the floor. It was just as he had practiced for weeks with the ball.

Jack recalls being transfixed, watching the drama unfold as a surreal slow-motion picture. Then, crashing back to his senses, he yelled at Felix and bolted out of his chair to save Tweety from the biting jaws of Felix. He was too late, and most of the evidence had been swallowed by the time he got to the scene of the crime.

By now, Grandma had a broom and rushed toward Felix. In an instant, she morphed from a grandma in an apron into an angry hockey player. She chased Felix around the house with the broom, and finally caught him with a slap shot, as he was clinging to the backdoor screen.

Felix hit the floor running, and scrambled under the kitchen table with Grandma in hot pursuit. Jack opened the door, and Felix darted out as Grandma missed with her last swing. She followed that with an oath and an admonition that Felix was no longer welcome inside.

As for young Jack, who looked more like the proverbial cat that ate the canary than the one who actually did eat it, she told him he should never have been playing inside with the fishing pole in the first place.

After a few days, Jack resumed *cat fishing* with Felix when grandma wasn't around. Apparently, he wasn't really as contrite as he acted on the day his tomfoolery led to Tweety's demise.

As for Grandma, she eventually forgave Felix and things went back to normal, but without Tweety.

Spill the Milk, Not the Moonshine

SOMETIME IN 1962, MY stepfather decided to make moonshine. It was never exactly clear to me what prompted his decision.

It wasn't out of necessity. Prohibition was repealed by the 21st Amendment in 1933, and Willow Springs had several retail outlets that sold liquor: Ousley's Package Store across from the Daisy Queen, both drugstores, and the package store adjacent to the Aztec Club, a "set-up" restaurant, on the outskirts of town.

A footnote: As a matter of law back then, the sale of liquor by the drink for consumption on the premises of a bar or restaurant was generally not available except in larger towns. To get around this, restaurants would allow patrons to bring their own booze, but charge them for glasses, ice, and mixers—set-ups.

Nor, was his motivation a matter of money. He had no intention of selling it, and as a retired naval officer, he could buy liquor at discounted rates in the commissary at Fort Leonard Wood on his regular trips there.

And it certainly wasn't because he was concerned that people would know that he drank distilled spirits. Anybody that knew

George Rothwell, also knew he didn't give two hoots what some-one else might think about his behavior. Even if he did, some of the aforementioned businesses made discrete home deliveries.

Incidentally, "two hoots" is not how he would have expressed his disdain. He would have used more dramatic and colorful language, which any sailor would understand.

He wasn't a problematic drinker. In fact, during the 17 years I knew him, I never once saw him intoxicated. Even in the two taverns he ran, he would only, as he put it, "graze" on a beer while he served customers. His drink of choice was strong, black coffee.

Why, then, did he want to make moonshine? I think he just wanted to see if he could do it. He once decided to make potato chips instead of buying them for his tavern. That experiment, according to my mother, was an abject failure and as imprac-tical as making marshmallows at home, when they could be purchased in bags at the grocery store.

Where did he get the still? That I can answer. A local county sheriff, who will remain anonymous, busted up a moonshine operation and confiscated two stills, a 40-gallon, square one, and a 10-gallon, "little cutie." Both were copper, and presumably would prevent one from going blind, from consuming the product.

I was not supposed to know about the stills, but it was hard to hide them in the two-bedroom house, which no longer exists, at 705 High Street. My impression was they were just novelties. Nevertheless, they were covered with a blanket in the storage room, which was a converted garage.

I learned from my mother that in preparation, George had gone to Mtn. View and West Plains to surreptitiously purchase corn and sugar for the mash. Whatever his motivation, he was a man on a mission.

During this period of time, we bought milk from J.E. Hill, the father of Eddie Mack, Eric, and Beverly, and stepfather to Jayne, Gene, Terry, and Wanda LeBaron.

J.E. was an employee of the Missouri Highway Department in Willow, but had acquired some cows, and was pedaling milk on the side.

Several times a week, before he went to his day-job at the Highway Department, he would leave a gallon jar of milk on our porch, and pick up an empty jar from the previous delivery.

One morning, I was awakened to J.E.'s pounding on my bedroom window. "Hey, Lonnie. Wake up. I need a jar. You didn't leave a return jar on the porch."

In those days of high teenage melatonin levels, I didn't wake up easily. J.E. kept pounding on my window, and I finally got the message. He needed a gallon jar.

I got out of bed and clomped half-asleep into the kitchen in search a jar. Seeing nothing on the counter, I looked underneath the sink, and back in the corner, I spied a gallon jar full of water.

I dumped the water into the sink, took the jar to J.E., and went back to bed.

Later that morning, I noticed a suspiciously calm atmosphere at the breakfast table. Not the usual chitchat that accompanied morning coffee. Something was up, but I was clueless.

As I was about to leave for school, Mom caught me at the front door. "What did you do with that jar underneath the sink?"

"It was full of water, and I poured it out because J.E. needed a jar."

She shook her head and told me I had dumped out a gallon of 150-proof white lightning that George had spent all night cooking. He was, no doubt, livid but couldn't complain because I wasn't supposed to know about it.

She warned me not to say anything, and I never mentioned the incident, and neither did George. I don't know if he ever made another batch, but if he did, I'm sure he didn't hide the results under the sink.

I often wondered what J.E. Hill thought when he unscrewed the lid on the jar that I gave him that morning. Now, I doubt he smelled anything. Ethyl alcohol, without flavoring or additives, has little odor until it is metabolized after consumption.

And, as far as I know, George never cried over the spilled moonshine.

FFA: A Proud Tradition at WSHS

FOR THE RECORD, I was never a member of the Future Farmers of America. Nor, did I take any Vocational Agriculture classes, as I didn't anticipate being a farmer, but I respected the FFA and my friends who were members.

In my mind's eye, I still see those boys in their distinctive blue jackets emblazoned with the gold FFA emblem and their names embroidered on the front. They wore those jackets with as much pride as anyone who wore a varsity letter jacket; and some of them wore both.

Although I didn't see farming in my future, it was certainly part of my past. As I have mentioned in previous articles, my brother Jack and I lived with our grandparents on a 40-acre, rocky-top Shannon County farm in the 1950s. We raised cows, pigs, turkeys, guineas, ducks, and farmed an acre-plus garden.

My grandfather's left arm had been amputated above the wrist years before in a blacksmith shop accident, yet, he tilled the garden behind a plow pulled by our horse, Dolly.

When Grandpa worked, he wore a prothesis with a mechanical hook that he could operate by manipulating its leather shoulder harness. His technique was barely noticeable. With his hook clamped on one handle of the plow and his right hand gripped on the other, he would call to the horse in traditional language of muleskinners, "Gee, Dolly" or "Haw, Dolly," and the horse would respond and veer right or left.

It was a sad day when Dolly died. Particularly, for my brother . . . he had to take Dolly's place. Grandpa tied a rope around Jack's waist and hitched it to the plow and called out directions as before: "Gee, Jack." and "Haw, Jack." Any psychological scars this might have caused Jack were, no doubt, erased by the United States Marine Corps.

My farm education continued during the summers after my sophomore and junior years, working in the Kansas wheat harvest. Twelve hours driving a 1933 John Deer tractor pulling a four-bottom plow behind a combine, and then driving a two-ton truck loaded with wheat to the grain elevator 20 miles away, made for long days.

And when it was too wet to plow, mucking out pig manure, while battling the largest flies this side of the Amazon, to spread on a pasture was hardly a welcome treat.

So, now, you know why I didn't see farming in my future, but since it is FFA week, I wanted to establish my farm creds before commenting.

Back in my day, FFA membership consisted mostly of farm boys in high school taking vo-ag classes, but that's changed. Membership is no longer just a pathway for future production farmers. According to its national website, the official name is now the National FFA Organization. The 1988 name change reflects " . . .the growing diversity and new opportunities in the industry of agriculture [and] welcomes members who aspire to careers as teachers, doctors, scientists, business owners and more."

Now, and back then, the FFA extracurricular activities enhanced leadership, business, and social skills. They elected officers, and other members had assigned responsibilities for their various projects.

My classmate, Ed Cauldwell, was elected president of the local chapter in 1964. Ed joined our class in the 8th grade along with Sophus Collins, Robert Gossard, Jimmy Johnson, and a host of others when some of the country schools like Noblett consolidated with Willow.

With his even temperament and friendly nature, it is not surprising the members chose Ed for the position. Unfortunately, Ed passed away in 1997. His health deteriorated over a period of many years, after his military service in Vietnam.

As part of their business training, and to earn money for their projects, the FFA boys sold popcorn at football and basketball games.

It wasn't all business, however. The chapter held an annual Parent-Son Banquet, with awards given for "Chapter Farmer" and "Greenhand." In my seventh-grade year, the Future Farmers hosted the FHA girls (Future Homemakers of America) at a roller-skating party. I still find that as impressive as any college mixer, but of course, in those days dancing was not allowed at a school event.

WSHS had a strong FFA chapter in the 1960s, often with over 60 members, and it was led by longtime sponsor and teacher, Lindell Pigg.

I remember Mr. Pigg being as kind and gentle as TV actor Mr. Rogers, but in World War II, he left high school to join the army, and was wounded in France when a grenade was thrown in his tank. He received a purple heart and spent a year in rehab.

After the war, he earned an A.B. in Agriculture Education and a Master of Education from the University of Missouri. He began teaching in Willow in 1956, and taught Vocational Agriculture I, II, III, and IV. He was also the father of schoolmates, Dick, Don, and Patricia Pigg.

With Mr. Pigg's guidance, the FFA members made formidable showings in area competitions. In 1961, members garnered 47 ribbons at the Heart of the Ozarks Howell County Fair. Ian Kurtz won 24 ribbons and Jerry Brummet collected 10.

Today, the National FFA Organization represents not just farmers of the future, but the " . . . the Future Biologists, Future Chemists, Future Veterinarians, Future Engineers and Future Entrepreneurs of America, too."

Last week, I got an email from a college friend saying his Ag-Econ degree took him to 48 states and over 70 countries. It seems the future is promising for Future Farmers.

Perhaps, I should have taken some of those vocational-ag classes.

Jacks Fork: A River for Floating, Swimming, and Baptizing

THE JACKS FORK, ACCORDING to the Missouri Department of Conservation, " . . .is named after John Jacks, a Shawnee Indian, who settled near the headwaters of the river in the 1830s." I never knew that. I suppose I thought it was named after a hillbilly who had the temerity to homestead there. But what I do know, the Jacks Fork is a place of beauty and vivid memories.

Now, part of the Ozark National Scenic Riverways, the Jacks Fork River starts at the Prongs, a few miles northwest of Mtn. View, where the North Prong and the South Prong converge. In my day, we called the convergence the Forks.

According to the Missouri Department of Natural Resources website, "The North Prong has its beginnings approximately 9 miles south of Raymondville . . . while the headwaters of the South Prong are located approximately 5 miles east of Cabool. . .." From the Prongs, it flows almost 50 miles easterly, where it joins the Current River 5.5 miles northeast of Eminence. (Source: U.S. Geologic Survey)

I learned to swim in the Jacks Fork at Ratcliff Ford, the first good swimming hole west of the Highway 17 bridge. You knew you were an accomplished swimmer, when the adults would let you swim across to the bluff on the far side to get a drink of the spring water that flowed out of the bluff.

Ratcliff Ford remains one of my favorite spots. It isn't surprising that in the 1950s and 1960s some prominent Mtn. View families had cabins there: Penninger (grocery store) and Castle (movie theater.) Once, when a friend and I pulled ashore during a rainstorm, Shorty Castle and his wife invited us inside for coffee.

In high school, I floated from the Prongs to the Highway 17 bridge dozens of times, often with Royce Yardley (WSHS Class of '66), in a fiberglass canoe that he and his father Lee Yardley had made. The canoe was lighter, wider, and more stable than an average canoe. The width gave it greater water displacement and buoyancy, perfect for scooting over the shallow rapids between the deeper holes. Moreover, unlike a narrower canoe, it was hard to swamp and could accommodate a bunch of camping gear.

We would often camp along the way, picking a spot with an elevated bank or gravel bar, with a deep swimming hole and a tall bluff. We never had much luck fishing, but had great fun jumping off 40-foot bluffs. I recall the fear just before jumping, but with my buddies around, I couldn't back out, and pride went before the fall. Still, all the way down it seemed like a bad idea, until I hit the water and surfaced with the exhilaration of a proud daredevil.

Today, the thought of jumping from that height is frightening. I don't even like climbing ladders. My present fear was galvanized two years ago when I foolishly climbed on a land-scaping boulder to trim a tree limb and ended up on the ground with a broken collarbone.

The Jacks Fork was also the site of my first baptism, but a little background information is in order.

My religious instruction began in 1956 in Montier, which is about halfway between Mtn. View and Birch Tree. Back then, Montier had two crossroad country stores on either side of old Highway 60. Incidentally, one of the stores, Longnecker's, was owned by the parents of current Willow Springs residents, Jo Anne Taylor and Janie Webb. The town also boasted a one-room post office, a scattering of houses, a 19th century community hall, a cemetery, a two-room school, and two churches—A Methodist and the Church of God of Prophecy.

From my perspective at the time, the Methodists were a bit calmer in their services, but most everyone I knew went to the Church of God of Prophecy, and it, too, was calm . . . until the preaching started. In retrospect, it is odd because the pastor, Reverend Fuller, was a mild-mannered, rather quiet man. That is, until he got behind the pulpit.

Now, and I mean no disrespect, when I hear Neil Diamond's 1969 song, "Brother Love's Traveling Salvation Show," I think fondly of Reverend Fuller, with his rhythmic cadence and bursts of tonal inflections, while mischievous kids in the back pews surreptitiously passed notes.

Between Reverend Fuller's preaching and that of an out-of-town evangelist at a brush arbor revival at Montier, a half-dozen youngsters made professions of faith. The following

February—yes, February— the church announced that the unchristened converts would be baptized in the Jacks Fork.

Jacks Fork River at Missouri Highway 17 bridge between Mountain View and Summersville. *Photo courtesy of Lee Kern fllog.floatblog@gmail.com.*

On a blustery Sunday afternoon in the middle of February, the other pilgrims and I arrived at Jacks Fork near the Highway 17 bridge just north of Mountain View. A towering limestone bluff, with an ancient, gnarled cedar protruding near the top, shadowed the pristine water there—a place worthy of the sacrament.

A gathering of church and family members sang the traditional baptizing hymn, "Shall We Gather at the River," as Reverend Fuller stood waist deep in the water, and beckoned us, one by one, to join him and be baptized in the name of the Father, Son, and Holy Ghost.

The Lord, notwithstanding, Jacks Fork was frigid in February, although it would have seemed blasphemous at the time to admit it.

When I moved to Willow Springs, most of my friends went to the Baptist church, so I did, too. I began singing in the choir, and during a revival, Sandra West, now my sister-in-law, told me I ought to join the church. It sounded like a good idea, but I didn't realize that carried with it another baptism.

It seemed to me one was sufficient, but the powers-that-be, namely, my stepfather thought otherwise. And he had been at my Jacks Fork baptizing. He wasn't a regular church-goer, but he had donated $500 to the building fund when the First Baptist Church in Willow was constructed. Perhaps, he was looking for a return on his investment. The second time, Brother Floyd Gentry did the dunking.

According to a friend of mine, whose father was a minister, two baptizings wasn't all that dramatic. He said he had been born again so many times his soul had stretchmarks.

In 1993, at my mother's funeral at First Baptist in Willow, my wife asked me what was behind the drapes back of the choir loft. I told her it was a small swimming pool. She did not believe me, so after the service I showed her. She's Catholic, and they don't do full emersion.

Nothing restores my country soul more than a visit to Jacks Fork.

Richie and The Fonz

I FIRST MET TRUMAN Grogan the summer of 1959, the summer before the seventh grade, when I moved to Willow Springs. We met playing baseball and became best friends. And remained friends for the rest of his life.

A lot of guys considered Truman their best friend. Guys named Eddie Mack Hill, Bill Tandy, John McGlynn, and Tom Siegrist. Truman had a style and personality about him that attracted people.

If you are familiar with the TV series *Happy Days*, I was Richie Cunningham, but he was The Fonz, hip, slick, and cool but without a motorcycle or a car. In fact, his elderly parents didn't own a car. They lived on South Center Street, across the railroad tracks, in a part of town everyone called "Death Valley."

Although the school yearbooks have photos of Truman in a suitcoat and tie, none of the coats were his—they were all borrowed for the occasion.

But growing up in Willow Springs, you weren't judged by your parents' wealth, not that many were wealthy, but rather, by who you were as an individual; whether you were a good teammate; or how you performed as a student.

I lived with the Grogans for several months two different times when I was in high school. Our freshman year, when my mother spent 9 months in Fitzsimmons Army Hospital, and our junior year, when my mother went to beauty school. I never met two more generous folks than his parents, Frank and Iva Grogan.

Truman was the best natural athlete that I ever played with or against in high school sports, and it always seemed effortless for him.

In Babe Ruth League baseball in 1959, Truman struck out 13 batters in one game, and the games only lasted seven innings. That's nearly two strikeouts an inning. Truman's athleticism so impressed a coach from a neighboring town that he paid his way to the Mickey Owen summer baseball camp.

An outstanding basketball player, Truman lettered all 4 years in high school. It is a notable achievement when you're good enough to play varsity basketball as a freshman, and it wasn't because we lacked talented upperclassmen.

But his most formidable athletic ability, until he injured his back in a car wreck in high school, may have been in track. It was evident even in junior high when he qualified for the Junior Olympics in the quarter and half-mile runs.

He had talent, but his training habits left something to be desired. Truman was a picky eater. He did not like green vegetables, but he loved hamburgers and fried chicken, which he would eat before track meets. Invariably, he threw up between races.

Once, on the day of a track meet, Coach Buddy Bennett took Truman to his home for lunch to keep Truman from eating hamburgers. He offered him some healthier choices that Truman refused to eat. Coach finally gave up and left Truman's stomach issues to Truman.

In junior high track, Truman nearly always won first place in the half and quarter-mile events. During a track meet with Mtn. Grove, Truman overheard the Mtn. Grove coach tell his star half-miler "to let Grogan set the pace."

Truman Grogan on the left; Lonnie Whitaker in the center; and Gary Evans at the edge, in front of Fergusons Drugstore in Willow Springs, after summer baseball practice in 1961. *Photo courtesy of Dan Zimmerman and the Willow Springs News.*

Truman decided to beat them at their own game. He told me he could outsprint their guy, so he set the pace by jogging the first of two laps, and the Mtn. Grove boy dutifully followed his coach's orders and trailed behind Truman.

Both coaches started yelling for them to pick up the speed, but Truman, with a big grin on his face, kept up his leisurely pace until the last hundred yards. Then he put on a burst of speed and won the race, not in a fast time, but with a sizeable lead ahead of the Mtn. Grove boy.

In my view, however, Truman's most spectacular footrace, witnessed only by my brother Jack and me, occurred one evening when his older brother, Tony, and Jack were home on leave from the Marine Corps.

Tony Grogan, fueled by more than a couple beers, argued that he was faster in the quarter mile than Truman. The argument led to a challenge that resulted in the Grogan brothers at the Palenske Field track around midnight. Tony in cowboy boots and Truman in loafers.

Under the light of a partial moon, they shot off from the starting line. We lost sight of them as they rounded the first curve, but could see them across the field, neck and neck, at the halfway mark. Coming into the final turn, we could hear them breathing hard, with Tony in the lead.

Tony finished ahead, but the argument continued. Truman complained that his shoes kept slipping off. Tony countered that he was in cowboy boots. Jack and I just laughed.

In the early 1960s, Truman and I rode the bus from Willow Springs to St. Louis. His sister Frankie (Beaird) had gotten baseball tickets for us to see our first Cardinal's game. And it was a doozy—the San Francisco Giants vs. the Cards, with Juan Mariscal and Bob Gibson, two of the fiercest competitors in baseball, pitching.

We saw Willie Mays and Willie McCovey hit back-to-back home runs; Kenny Boyer and Dick Groat hit home runs; and witnessed Willie Mays miss a fly ball in center field. We also learned that Frankie's favorite player was Tim McCarver. It's a trip we relived countless times.

I've focused on Truman's athletic ability, but what some people don't know, he was a voracious reader. In fact, that summer before the 7th grade, he taught me how to use the library. He recommended various books he had read. Truman, over his life, read more books than practically anybody I know. After he read my first novel, and said it was pretty good for a first book, I took it as high praise.

Truman's story isn't one of a high school star whose best years and only accomplishments were as a teenager. He parlayed the skills he learned working summers in Oklahoma with his electrician uncle into a career in electronics. He married Sandy Merrill, the girl he loved in high school, and raised two daughters.

At his memorial service a few weeks ago, I had an interesting conversation with his 3-foot something, granddaughter, Hannah, who is a fan of my children's book, *Mulligan Meets the Poodlums*.

She approached me and asked if I was the person who had written her Mulligan book. I said that I was. She beamed, as if I were a celebrity. Then she said, "You must be rich." I asked her why she thought that. She said, "You look rich." I had on a suit and tie. Then she said, "I'll bet your shoes cost $75." I said one of them did. She ignored my cleverness.

"How much did your shoes cost?" I asked. She told me hers cost $45. Now, I was impressed. Hers had sequins and unicorns.

"Do you live in a mansion?" she asked. I told her I lived in a house. "Does your house have mansions in it?" It wasn't until the service started that I realized the source of the question: "In my father's house are many mansions." Smart girl.

She wanted to know if people wanted my autograph. I told her they didn't—they just wanted books signed. At this point, I think she was becoming less enamored by me, because she wanted to know if I knew any famous authors.

I told her I knew Johnny Boggs. "What does he write?" she asked. I told her that Johnny wrote Westerns. Almost gleeful, she said, "I'll bet my grandpa had one of his books." I told that as a matter of fact he did, and that Johnny had signed it for him. Now, she was impressed. And somewhere, Truman smiled.

In the end, our stories are our legacy, and we keep loved ones alive in our hearts when we tell their stories.

Montier's Favorite Actor

HAVE YOU SEEN THE Hearing Assist TV commercial with the son attempting to talk to his hearing-impaired father, and then the father goes into a monologue pitch for a hearing aid, followed by the son's tagline, "I love you, Dad."?

Or, perhaps, you've seen the GEICO/Helzberg Diamonds TV spot with the iconic gecko (a lizard, for Ozarkers) approaching a beach wedding, with a distinguished-looking minister presiding.

Well, I've seen both commercials numerous times. But the first time I saw the GEICO commercial, I was sitting on the couch with my wife, watching the gecko approach the beach wedding, and did a doubletake at the wedding scene. "Hey, Mary Ellen, I went to grade school with that minister." And in the doubting voice she employs when she thinks I'm up to something, said, "Oh, you did not."

"No, really." I explained that Robert Shepherd, the actor playing the minister, was a schoolmate at the two-room, country school in Shannon County (Montier).

Before long, I began seeing him as the main actor and pitch-man in the nationally broadcast hearing aid commercial. And when Wal-Mart displays a Hearing Assist poster of you on its shelves, for sure, a country boy has "arrived."

In addition to TV commercials, plays, and trade films, he has appeared in numerous movies, including *Evan Almighty*, *The Book of Ruth*, and *Mary for Mayor*, and has hung out with actors such as Scott Glenn (*The Right Stuff, Urban Cowboy*) and Corbin Bernsen (*LA Law, Major League*).

In the movie *Lincoln*, Shepherd portrayed the doctor who pronounced Academy Award-winner Daniel Day Lewis dead. I saw the movie, and at the time, had no idea it was Robert Shepherd.

In the third season of the TV miniseries, *Legend and Lies*, he had a featured role, appearing in all twelve episodes, as Secretary of War Edwin Stanton. It was stunning how much he resembled this historic figure and captured the intensity of the times with his performance.

All his connections made me curious. Based the Kevin Bacon parlor game, how many degrees of separation existed between him and Kevin Bacon? It turns out he was an extra in the Kevin Bacon film *Hollow Man*, which means there is only one degree separating me from Kevin. Who knew?

Robert currently resides in Virginia, but I connected with him on Facebook, and asked if he would be interested in being profiled in the *Howell County News*. He said it sounded like fun. So, let me tell you more about the actor from Montier.

Robert Shepard, still known as Bob to family and friends, was raised on farm in Shannon County, a couple miles down the gravel road from my grandparents' farm. We attended the same church, and I actually have a vivid memory of sitting next to him at a brush arbor revival.

Actor Robert Shepherd at a riding stable preparing for a role. *Photo courtesy of Robert Shepherd.*

Bob was two grades ahead of me at the Montier school, and for 4 years we rode the same school bus, but after the sixth grade I moved to Willow Springs, and Bob went on to graduate from Birch Tree High School.

Wondering what he was like in high school, I asked Judy Mizer Barnes, another BTHS alum, who still resides in Birch Tree, what she remembered about Bob. "He was our Band Major, and wore a beautiful uniform with a tall hat. Boy, could he march. He led our band in parades, with three girls as majorettes, of which I was one. He was one of the boys who was as much a friend to girls as boys. Mannerly and thoughtful, always. Just an all-around good person."

Did he always want to be an actor? Bob says, "I can't remember when I didn't want to be an actor, but was not sure how to get there." He participated in Christmas programs at church and the Montier School, which he says "were something I excitedly looked forward to. I had the lead in our junior-year play and played the villain in the senior play." He added that "singing both at church and high school helped to expand my performing options."

Incidentally, I last saw Bob my sophomore year at the district music contests in Rolla, when he competed in the vocal solo category singing "Give a Man a Horse He Can Ride." (What can I say? I remember the oddest things.) Ironically, although Bob grew up on a cattle farm, he wasn't an equestrian and took riding lessons for a role that required him to mount a horse.

After graduating from Southwest Missouri State (now, Missouri State), Bob returned home to teach the sixth grade at Birch Tree, and later, taught at Liberty. He taught from August 1967 to December 1971.

His national TV debut occurred during the summer of 1970 on *The Dating Game*. While visiting his aunt in California, he auditioned at a casting call for the popular TV show. Remarkably, he had never seen the show before, since TV reception was still unavailable on his family farm. In fact, to see the show when it aired after he returned home in August, he went to the local banker's house.

Not only did Bob beat out 200 other wannabe panelists for *The Dating Game*, he won the date. You may recall that the "bachelors" were kept out of sight from the contestants, who could only hear the responses to their questions. Apparently,

Bob's rich baritone voice and extemporaneous acting ability served him well.

His acting career, however, took a circuitous route. After teaching for several years, he entered graduate school, returned to ROTC and earned a Regular Army commission that led to a 22-year career and meeting his wife, Marcia.

Bob's first paid acting gig occurred while on active duty in Fort Campbell, KY. He snagged a featured extra role in Robert Altman's *Nashville*, which was shot on location in Nashville, approximately 40 miles south of the Fort.

Bob contacted the movie production office and indicated he would like to work on the film. Later, a producer called asking if he would show actor Scott Glenn around the Fort, as he had been cast as a soldier in the 101st Airborne. Of the experience, Bob says, "So, Scott came up on the bus and I escorted him around the post. My wife and I drove him back to Nashville. We were both cast as extras for the race car scene."

Robert and his father Jim Shepherd at the family farm in Montier, Missouri, circa 1965. *Photo courtesy of Megan Shepherd Fluhart-Montano.*

But like most professional artists and actors, Bob has paid his dues. After three years in the army, he resigned his Regular Army commission in 1976 to pursue his acting dream in California. "We were living on a shoestring and expecting our first child, which we had saved up for the delivery bill. Ten days after our daughter's birth, Marcia had an aneurysm and was in ICU for two weeks before surgery. After which, she was miraculously healed and had no residual effects. But we were in debt $14,000 with no steady job, so we moved back to the Ozarks where I almost immediately started teaching in the Liberty School System."

It wasn't the end of his dream, however. Bob says, "In the hospital, while still in LA, I distinctly heard a voice in my head: 'Delay is not denial.'"

After two more years teaching, Bob returned to the military and ultimately retired. Of his retirement he says, "Then, I could afford to be a freelance actor. I got an agent and started booking jobs and have been doing so for almost 30 years."

It seems so many people want to be actors but fail. I asked him for the secret to his success. His answer reflects his humility: "I believe if there is a secret to being a working actor, it is to never give up. Rejection is ever present. Also, never think a role is too small or unimportant. So, I have worked on student films, training films, and ultra-low budget features. Even roles that did not pay. I have heard and believe: 'Do what is in front of you and the rest will take care of itself.'"

As a follow-up question, I asked how he got his acting jobs. "There are multiple ways to find acting jobs. I currently work with three talent agents. However, I have been in the business a long time so many times I am contacted directly. Also, jobs come up on Face Book and the internet to apply for."

Toward the end of our discussion, I asked if there was something he would lie readers to know, and he provided a hopeful message. "What I would like readers to know is 'Delay is not Denial.'"

For more information on Bob, go online to https://www.imdb.com/.

Church Camp Confidential

DURING THE SUMMERS OF 1960 – 1962, as a First Baptist kid in Willow Springs, the church camp near Van Buren, Missouri, highlighted the summer.

If you experienced camping there, no doubt, you have your own memories. Perhaps, a moving experience at the sunrise and vesper services at Inspiration Point. But if you are like me, you remember the fun: talent shows, the Nibble Nook, swimming, staying up all night—as Talbird Lovan (WSHS Class of '68) remembers, "That was when I was able to go without sleep for a week."

But politics? Boys bleaching their hair? Attacks by blister-causing vectors? Arms in slings? Or, the "Barnyard Charleston?" And all under the watchful eyes of preachers and counselors? Surely not. Well, maybe.

The South Missouri Baptist Assembly (SMBA) still operates a camp at the site, but the camp of my experience has under-gone significant remodeling. In the sixties, most churches had their own residential cabins with dining rooms, and none had air-conditioning. Now, individual church cabins are mostly gone, and campers stay in two large, air-conditioned dormitories.

According to the SMBA website, the camp now offers " . . . many recreation opportunities, including a swimming pool, basketball and volleyball courts . . .and more." For recreation during my time (I'm beginning to sound like a grumpy old man boasting about trudging 5 miles in the snow to school), campers hiked down a gravel path and swam in the Current River (boys and girls separately, of course). Or we played ping-pong in the Nibble Nook, a screened-in rec room/snack shop, which was the social gathering point of the camp.

Inspiration Point overlooking the Current River at the Baptist Church Camp near Van Buren, Missouri. *Photo courtesy of Jenny Hale Pigg.*

In the rustic setting of the Ozark hills, medical emergencies weren't uncommon. I remember waking up around 2 a.m. with a burning sensation on my throat. I stumbled to the bathroom to look in the mirror and saw a water-filled blister the size of a quarter. Not knowing what to do, I padded back to bed and fell asleep. When I got out of bed later that morning, I discovered the one big blister was now nine smaller ones that burned like the dickens.

The camp nurse informed me I had been bitten by a blister bug and that wherever the fluid inside the blister ran it would create a new blister. She drained the blisters, dabbed them with alcohol—ouch—and wrapped my neck with gauze, which gave me a gauze turtleneck. I wasn't the only blister bug victim. At the sunrise service, I saw a girl with a blister on her arm the size of a fifty-cent piece.

Until a couple years ago, I wondered if the nasty creatures still existed, when I found this suspicious-looking blister on my little toe and had a flashback to 1961. So, I drained it ever so carefully, making sure none of the fluid escaped. I wasn't careful enough and ended up with a second blister. I mentioned this to my dermatologist, who said he had never heard of such a thing. City Folks!

But the worst injury happened to Jenny Hale Pigg (WSHS Class of '68), when she fell while hiking and gashed her elbow on a rock. It was a nasty wound, but she was a trooper. Jody Corn (WSHS Class of '65) was nearby at the time and wrapped a cloth around the cut to control the bleeding. Nevertheless, Mr. and Mrs. Hale came and took her to a doctor in Van Buren where she got 10 stiches. Jenny still remembers the date—Wednesday, June 21, 1961—and still has the scar.

The camping experience wasn't without politics. The staff divided campers into two separate parties—the Nibblers and the

Snackers. After each party selected king and queen candidates, the campaign started. In 1961, Willow Springs was part of the Snackers party, which nominated Bill Tandy (WSHS Class of '64) as its king candidate.

The campaign involved a flurry of activity, with signs, posters, stump speeches, and a bit of political chicanery—Bill changed the sign on the Nibble Nook to "Snackers' Cranny." Our enthusiasm prevailed, and we crowned Bill as the camp king.

It wasn't surprising that Bill won the election. He had charisma and a certain star-quality aura. But, apparently, he felt he needed more. Maybe, something more—such as blond hair like Dobie Gillis, the popular TV star. Bill conned me into going with him to the drugstore in Van Buren to buy hydrogen peroxide.

Afterwards, he turned on his Tom Sawyer charm and convinced Truman Grogan and Eddie Mack Hill (both WSHS Class of '65) to join him in the experiment. Although clueless about the process, the three of them, nevertheless, ended up towheads, and they definitely got the desired attention from girls.

Ping pong tournaments in the Nibble Nook were ongoing, and Tandy was the usual winner. But then a local gunslinger, a table tennis whiz from Van Buren, Lynn Spence (WSHS Class of '64), arrived on the scene, and a showdown was inevitable.

With bragging rights on the line, Lynn and Bill squared off in the championship match, surrounded by onlookers inside the Nibble Nook. Others observed from outside through the screen windows. Of the match, Bill says, "I remember playing Spence but can't recall who won. I recall Lynn always had his tongue hanging out the corner of his mouth when stressed." I remember watching the playoff that day, but can't remember the winner either.

First Baptist had its own cabin that could accommodate 40 boys and girls. Shaped like a World War II military barracks, it had a wall down the center that partitioned the girls from the boys.

The entrance had a foyer, with chaperone bedrooms on either side. In my day, it was Pastor Floyd Gentry for the boys and Pansy Belle Hord for the girls. Each side had separate bathrooms. Underneath, a walk-in basement housed the kitchen and dining room, where all meals were eaten.

The knotty pine wall separating the two sides allegedly had a couple miniscule holes. One day, Bill Tandy stood on his bunk, which was adjacent to the wall, exploring for the opening. His enthusiasm equaled that of a prospector searching for the Lost Dutchman's Mine. From the way he was dancing on his bed, he had struck gold. His enthusiasm was short-lived.

He didn't realize that a silence had come over the room. But he stopped dancing when a hand rested on his shoulder—Pastor Gentry's. "Bill, what are you doing? The barnyard Charleston?" Without turning around, Bill slid down the wall and covered up with his blanket. The room exploded with laughter, and the wall exploration ended . . . at least from the boys' side.

Church camp would not have been the same without Pastor Floyd Gentry—nearly everyone referred to him as Brother Gentry. I always held him in high regard, but have often thought he handled the wall incident deftly. Others in his position might have tried to inflict shame or embarrassment, which in my view, would have been the wrong course. Instead, he used humor to make his point.

In case you were wondering, Brother Gentry came to First Baptist Church in Willow March 1, 1953, from the First Baptist Church in Wheaton, MO. According to an old First Baptist Church bulletin, he was born and raised in Howell County, and received his education and training at several colleges, including Southwest Missouri State, Union University, and Central Baptist Seminary.

Of the many church camp experiences, I suspect the burning cross ceremony is the most memorable for many. From Inspiration Point, situated high atop the river bluff, you can see a half-mile in the distance below to a bend in the Current River. It is at this point where a 10-foot cross was erected.

I had seen the burning cross the year before, but in 1961, two preachers drafted Tandy and me to assist with the set up. We traveled to town, picked up the cross, wrapped in burlap feed bags, along with a can of kerosene, and loaded it all in a johnboat a mile downstream. At the site, we soaked the burlap bags with kerosene and waited until dark and a flashlight signal from Inspiration Point to light the fire.

A single match was all it took to set the cross ablaze and light up the river valley proclaiming the glory of its meaning, as a shining beacon to Inspiration Point. And as the flames reflected off the water, the cross appeared even larger.

But as the saying goes, change is inevitable. Even with the new amenities, camp attendance from Willow isn't as popular today. I queried current First Baptist pastor, Joel Hinds, about this and he responded, "From my perspective, there are simply not as many students interested in church camp. I expect this is mostly due to a busy schedule of sports camps and ball games all summer, even for young students."

Of course, the times were different then, but if today's campers with their new amenities and swimming pool have any more fun that we did, I don't know how they can stand it.

My thanks to Carol Aldridge, Jenny Pigg, and Pastor Joel Hinds for their research assistance.

Mountain View on a Saturday

MOUNTAIN VIEW IN THE 1950s bustled with activity on Saturdays. It seemed the town doubled in size. Farm families from the surrounding countryside showed up to do their weekly shopping and socializing. Women in freshly-ironed, cotton dresses and men in clean jeans, or even khaki work trousers, usually reserved for Sundays, strolled the sidewalks stopping to chat when they met a neighbor or an old friend.

For me, it meant a 10-mile trip on old Highway 60 from the Montier farm. With Grandpa driving his 1948 Mercury, it took most of an hour. The blacktop was hilly and curvy, and Grandpa seldom drove faster than 40 miles per hour. If he saw someone driving faster, he would proclaim, "That guy's in a hurry . . . in a hurry to get to the undertaker."

And he wouldn't pass another car, except on the straight stretch near Teresita, where he would invariably pass any vehicle in front of us. He'd clinch the turning knob on the steering wheel, which he said was required for one-armed drivers, and whip out to the oncoming lane, with the foot-feed (accelerator) to the floor.

Grandma, a stout five-footer who could barely see over the dashboard, sat patiently on the passenger side, while I squirmed in the back seat in anticipation of the excitement ahead. During the week they might drive a mile to Welsh's Montier Grocery, for animal feed or bread—Holsum or Colonial, white only—but on Saturdays, they stocked up with supplies "in town."

With no parking meters in Mountain View, cars and pickups occupied spaces along the sidewalks for extended periods. I don't recall the constable, Pete Thompson, ever writing parking tickets. Grandpa usually parked on a side street near Duncan's Funeral Home, situated at 2nd Street and Elm, which intersected with Main (1st Street) a block south.

This parking spot was strategic because it was only a block from Garrett's store, which sold groceries and work clothing, and would be the last shopping spot of the day. Garrett's was important for another reason. Because Grandpa only had one hand, his right hand, buying gloves was a problem—they come in pairs—but Garrett's would sell him a single glove. A man, whom Grandpa never met, was missing his right arm and would purchase the other glove.

Main Street, then a Monopoly board of merchant stores, ran east to west, north of the Frisco railroad tracks, with a gravel parking area in between. Most of the businesses are gone, but they remain vivid in my memory.

Padgett's Hardware anchored the corner on Elm, next to Ray Tackitt's Western Auto, the source of my first non-hand-me-down baseball glove. Castle's movie theater always warranted a stop to check out the movie posters, but I don't recall ever going to a Saturday movie—a matter of time and expense. I had my first cherry coke at the soda fountain in Heuer's drugstore. And Grandma always shopped at Penninger's grocery, in part, because she liked visiting with one of the proprietors, Brownie Penninger,

After Grandpa parked the car, and Grandma provided instructions about my deportment and the frugal use of my pocket change, I was like a dog off leash. My usual first order of business was to find my best buddy, Larry Stover, a Montier school chum, and a likely spot to find him was outside the pool hall on Oak Street between 2nd and Main. We were both too young to go inside, but we would stare through the front window at men chalking up snooker cues, and if we were lucky, see our teacher Mr. Shockley playing pinochle with men at tables in the rear.

A half block south toward Main, N. Frank's used book and oddities shop was a regular stop, mainly, for the discounted comic books, which had the title on the cover stripped off. I was always curious why the titles of the covers had been removed. In later years, I learned, at least with paperback books, a stripped cover is returned to the publisher evidencing the book didn't sell and is being destroyed.

Another thing I remember about N. Frank's is that's where I perused a copy of Buck Nelson's paperback booklet, *My Trip to Mars, the Moon, and Venus.* Buck Nelson, a bib over-all-wearing farmer in his sixties, had a farm northwest of Mountain View and claimed to have been visited by extra-ter-restrial aliens (from Venus) who took him on an interplanetary trip in their flying saucer.

Buck started having Spacecraft Conventions during the summers that attracted several hundred people. In fact, my mother, stepfather, and I went to one in 1958, but to my chagrin we did not see a spacecraft. Now, I wished I had bought his book, but I had other plans for my fifty cents.

For Larry and me, a Saturday trip would not have been complete without browsing at the Ben Franklin 5&10, just a around the corner on Main. The dime store sold glassware, sewing notions, games, yo-yos, penny candy, and school supplies, including Big Chief tablets. Fifty cents could stretch a long way at the dime store. What could possibly go wrong there? Answer: The dime store sold peashooters.

Pea shooters are toy blowguns, basically, hollow plastic tubes the size of a large drinking straw, through which dried peas, twice the size of a BB, are projected. Just put a few peas in your mouth and blow them out through the tube at a target. They came without an operator's manual or regulatory warnings, but farm kids raised with .22 rifles and common sense, understood safety. We took seriously the proverbial admonition, "You could put an eye out with that . . . ."

Armed with blowguns and bags of peas, and proud as Amazon warriors, we left in search of targets. Weaving in and out of sidewalk traffic to the end of the block at Padgett's, we crossed Elm diagonally past Richard Brothers feed and grocery store, and continued a block south to a weeded area behind the sale barn.

In the rafters of the covered livestock stalls, we spotted a target. I've heard it said that a hornet's nest isn't interesting until you poke it. We were about to test that theory on a wasp nest—gray and paper-like, loaded with angry-looking reddish-orange wasps.

At first, we fired a series of single shots from a distance, without much success (a poor choice of words). Feeling braver, we moved closer and commenced a salvo of peas that must have connected . . . because it got very interesting. I still recall the pain from the sting on the top of my head, as I ran away from the vengeful swarm. Our gallant assault ended in a hasty retreat.

Main Street in Mountain View, Missouri in the 1950s.
Photo courtesy of Jeanne Sharp Gaddy.

However, I recall happier times at the sale barn. With Grandpa's assistance, I got to bid for and buy Henrietta, a Plymouth Rock hen, for less than a dollar. Henrietta came with a cage, so I kept her in my lap on the way home.

Henrietta may have been past her prime, but since I claimed her as a pet, she did not end up as Sunday dinner. I was quite proud, when to my grandparents' surprise, Henrietta actually laid an egg. That, I am sure we did eat.

Now, three decades have passed bringing inevitable change, but time has not passed Mountain View by. It has doubled in population and continues to be a commercial hub for the area. While Walmart and McDonalds on the north part of town have taken some of the bustle from Main Street, the buildings look much the same and provide nostalgia for those who remember the way they were.

Oklahoma . . . 59 Years Ago

FIFTY-NINE YEARS AGO, THE curtain went up for the WSHS production of Rogers and Hammerstein's *Oklahoma*. It was the first musical play in school history, and of my high school memories, it ranks near the top.

Oklahoma played to capacity crowds in the school auditorium November 16-17, 1961. Groups of observers came from Southwest Missouri State, Drury College, and surrounding towns.

The school yearbook, *Willamizzou*, devoted six full pages to the production that involved the combined efforts of the music, dramatics, and art departments, plus girls' physical education classes.

The mixed chorus class, instead of learning madrigals or other unfamiliar songs, rehearsed the title song, "Oklahoma," and other songs sung by the cast, including "The Surrey with the Fringe on Top," "Many a New Day," "Oh, What a Beautiful Morning," and "Kansas City," until pitch-perfect.

Under the supervision of art teacher Marie Booth, serving as sets and lighting director, art students wielded hammers, saws, and paint brushes to design and construct the stage sets, and later, behind the curtains, managed the scene changes during the performances.

The "surrey with the fringe on top" scene from the WSHS production of *Oklahoma. Photo is from the 1962 Willamizzou.*

Girls' physical education classes took a break from exercising with Indian clubs (wooden, bowling pin-looking-clubs) to practice dance routines for *Oklahoma*, under the direction of teacher Wilma Stringer. In the role of choreographer, Mrs. Stringer even managed to transform male cast members into formidable hoofers, combining a few steps from the Charleston with square dancing moves.

Junior Mary Nell Ladage and senior David Barnes headlined the show portraying sweethearts, Laurey and Curly. Mary Nell, the pretty Hoop Queen candidate and Bruin Band majorette, and David, the handsome athlete with curly hair and a resonant singing voice—he won first place in the state music competition—projected convincing on-stage chemistry.

Supporting actors, senior Janice Zimmerman and sophomore Bill Tandy, generated laughs playing mixed-up lovers, Ado Annie and Will Parker. Senior Gail McAllister wowed the crowds with her portrayal of the wise-cracking Aunt Eller. Sophomore Fred Corl nailed the part of Ali Hakim, the Persian peddler man, forsaking Ado Annie in favor of Gertie Cummings, played by senior Nancy Cowger, to avoid a "shotgun" wedding. And sophomore Sandra Davidson and senior Bill Haas tripped the light fantastic in the magical dream scene.

Bill Tandy recalls a scene that called for him to kiss a girl, but he was hesitant to do so because his good friend had a crush on the girl. When the time for the kiss arrived, he removed his cowboy hat and shielded their faces giving the appearance to the audience they were kissing. "I still regret not kissing her," Tandy says.

Junior Ron Frost played the villainous Jud Fry to perfection, with one slight problem—his singing voice was not equal to this thespian talents—and this was a musical. Music Director Carl Walker and the Art Department solved the problem.

For the famous bunkhouse scene, where Jud tries to frighten Curly, the set walls representing the inside of the bunkhouse, were painted to resemble rough-sawn boards, with a strategically placed knothole, a tad larger than a golf ball, about head high. During the performance, Mr. Walker hid behind the set and sang the words to "Poor Jud is Dead" through the knothole, while Ron pantomimed the words.

Although the main character parts had been previously selected in the spring semester, plenty of opportunities still existed for my freshman class in the fall. Sandy and Sharon Merrill, Peggy Henry, and Sandy Flake, became tutu-wearing dancehall girls behind the footlights. Eddie Mack Hill, Jody Corn, Jerry Brazeal, Richard Smith, and I donned borrowed cowboy boots and hats and strapped on shootin' irons and tried to keep pace with the girls' more graceful dancing moves.

Other classmates participated in offstage jobs. Doug James, Jim Thomas, the Zimmerman twins, and Barbara Graves worked the box office and served as ushers.

The arrival of music teacher Carl Walker and dramatics/ speech teacher Raimon Newby, within a year of each other, marked a fundamental change in dramatic arts at WSHS. Previously, the school had presented stage plays, but never a Broadway musical. And these two teachers had the chops to pull it off.

Both were musicians. Of course, you would expect that of Mr. Walker, with a Masters in Music Education from the University of Missouri, but he had also been a member of the select Mizzou University Singers.

As for Mr. Newby, he was no slouch as a singer. He earned extra money in college singing in a barbershop quartet, which actually made a record album. While in high school, I listened to the record, and it was good. Showing another example of his ability, he sang at the wedding of Barbara Sherrill and Dick Pigg (both, WSHS '64).

Together, the Walker/Newby collaboration paved the way for several musicals in the 1960s: *South Pacific, Carousel, and Annie Get Your Gun*. Deanna Collins (WSHS '64), a member for the *Oklahoma* cast, and who had the lead role in *South Pacific*, recently shared her memory of *Oklahoma*. "What a fun musical! Mr. Newby was a gifted director."

Trying to capture the smell of the greasepaint and roar of the crowd; the anticipation of opening night; the comradery of late school-night rehearsals; and the aura of excitement that existed in the school and town, is a hard task. Feelings and emotions are like that. But as to the memory of it all, Deanna Collins captured it nicely. "Those were wonderful, carefree days growing up in a safe community." And that's the way we were in the fall of 1961.

Mrs. Munford

CHANCES ARE, IF YOU went to Willow Springs High School from 1927 to 1967, you had Mrs. Jessie Munford as an English teacher. Even if you came afterwards, most likely you have heard stories about her.

I have previously described her as Jennifer Jones in the vintage movie Good *Morning, Miss Dove*, a teacher with an implied highhandedness that could put a smart aleck in his place by raising an eyebrow. Always impeccably dressed from stores in Springfield, her hair was never out of place.

Mrs. Jessie Munford. *Photo is from the 1965 Willamizzou.*

I recently queried class-mate Glenda Turner about her recollection of our teacher, and her description was nearly identical to mine. "Ah, Mrs. Munford . . . beautiful blue eyes peering over glasses that brought you in line without a single word. She was always impeccably dressed and coiffed."

Mrs. Munford arrived at WSHS, with her newly-acquired Bachelor of Science in Education from Central Missouri State College in 1927, along with her husband Ted. Over her long career she taught history, English, debate, speech, publications, and even physical education. But most of my generation remember her as the English teacher.

Recent phone calls from two longtime Willow Springs residents actually prompted this article. Marguerite Wehmer called me to talk about the article I had written about the Baptist Church Camp—she had gone there, too—in the 1940s. But as our conversation turned to all-things Willow Springs, I was surprised to learn she had also been a student of Mrs. Munford. A week later, Louise Gaulden called me and I learned that she, too, had Mrs. Munford as a teacher. I had gone to school with both ladies' children, and it got me to thinking.

I recall as clearly as if it were today, the first time I actually saw Mrs. Munford. Standing, with her ever-perfect posture on the WSHS auditorium stage, she was directing the *Willamizzou* photographer at the end of the 1959 Fall Fiesta ceremony. Phyliss Lovan and I were the 7th grade king and queen candidates.

Mrs. Munford arranged the student kings and queens just so for the perfect photo, and then in an imperial, theatrical voice, said "Smile, darn ya, smile." Incidentally, this phrase was the title of a 1931 movie cartoon, but for some reason, it annoyed my pre-teen self. Perhaps, it had to do with the lateness of the hour, or that my class had lost to Janice Corn and Randy James (both, WSHS '67).

The next morning when her name came up at the breakfast table, I spoke of her in unflattering terms, and my stepfather admonished me not to sound like him. Little did I know, Mrs. Munford would be my English teacher for the next five years, and that I would come to admire and appreciate her like few other teachers.

She wasn't touchy-feely or one to gush over your accomplishments. Helen Tandy, a former student, who returned to WSHS in 1961 to teach as a colleague of Mrs. Munford, says, "There weren't any funny things that happened in her classes. She was all business. I will just say, I was scared of her. However, I learned more from her than any teacher I ever had, even in college. I was so prepared for college and I owe it to her."

Personally, I can't say I was ever afraid of her, even in the 8th grade when my class had all high school teachers, but she demanded a standard of excellence. If she saw a culprit chewing gum, her response never varied— "park your gum." Even so, she would seamlessly ask an easy question of a shy student to allow him or her the opportunity to participate and give a correct answer.

At times I am surprised I did well in her classes. Elliot's Silas Marner made me catatonic. Bryant's poem Thanatopsis was beyond my ability to appreciate. The most significant thing I recall from Shakespeare's McBeth was classmates Annette Tetrick and Donna Spence reading the witches' parts out loud in class with impressive, shrill cackles. But I did okay in writing, because I applied her often-repeated mantra: there is no such thing as good writing—just good rewriting.

Nothing in my memory tops the assignment she gave us our freshman year. We were to write business letters seeking employment. As you might imagine, most were simple and unexciting. For example, Eddie Mack Hill wrote to his aunt for a summer lawn-mowing job. John McGlynn's letter, however, was a different matter. John, generally an "A" student, got a big fat "F" for a grammatically-perfect, error-free letter. Mrs. Munford took exception to his choice of employment.

John directed his letter to Hugh Heffner, the publisher of *Playboy* magazine, for the position of head photographer. In the letter, he advised Mr. Heffner that his lack of experience in photography would not be a problem because of his "enthusiasm." In addition to the big "F" marked in red, she wrote, "I don't appreciate corn." As an afternote, John went on to obtain a business degree from the University of Arkansas and went into the grocery business.

Mrs. Munford didn't suffer insubordination lightly. Mrs. Wehmer told me that once when she was a student, on the day of a test, Mrs. Munford told students to clear everything off their desks. In response, her classmate Ed Elmore dropped a stack of books on the floor making a loud boom. Mrs. Munford marched straight to his desk and slapped him across the face. Whether that incident led Ed to becoming a member of the Missouri Highway Patrol is not clear, but I gather on that day, it set him on the straight and narrow.

Although systematic and methodical in class, her personal life reflected a caring, considerate side. Noblesse oblige, a favorite precept of hers, refers to the obligation of anyone who is in a better position than others to act respectably and charitably. Over the years, she and her husband donated food and clothing to those in need, with little fanfare. Not surprisingly, the Willow Chamber of Commerce honored her with the Citizen of the Year award in 1960.

Working on the *Willamizzou* staff, which Mrs. Munford headed, I found her to be collegial and relaxed, and would even laugh at a clever joke. Glenda Turner, yearbook editor our senior year, said, "I would occasionally see her outside her 'professional' stance. On those occasions, she was a bit playful and nurturing. Looking back, I think she was one of the few older (at the time) women I truly admired. She was quite a beautiful human being." Another female classmate told me it was because of Mrs. Munford's encouragement that she finished college.

Mrs. Munford passed away in 1992. By the time I was born, she had been a teacher for twenty years. I can only imagine what it must have been like for her teaching the sons and daughters of her former students; seeing students march off to three major wars; or watching them become parents, teachers, schoolboard members, mayors, statewide office holders, judges, lawyers, doctors, a U.S. Congressman, or writers. But that is her legacy, and for some of us, she is part of ours.

"D" is for Determination

THE ARTICLES IN THIS column often mention my appreciation for the teachers and the education I received at Willow Springs. Learning was fun, and I was a mostly an A and B student. In fact, I received my first D in college. Well . . . that's not entirely true, so I will fess up to an incident involving venerable WSHS teacher Lorene Masnor.

Since many will be unfamiliar with Miss Masnor, a little background information is in order. She began teaching commercial studies at WSHS in 1930, but most students from my generation will remember her teaching bookkeeping, short-hand, and typing. As sophomores, when most of us took typing, she had been teaching for three decades.

It's fair to say, I think, that Miss Masnor was unique in a likeable, odd

Miss Lorene Masoner.
Photo is from the 1965 *Willamizzou.*

sort of way. A bit frumpy in her appearance, her dresses often clung where they should have draped. Ironically, her photograph in the 1939 *Willamizzou* presented a portrait of an attractive, well-groomed 20-something woman of the era.

According to neighbor Marguerite Wehmer, she was devoted to her elderly mother, whom she lived with in a house on East 7th Street. After her mother passed away, Miss Masnor could be seen driving her Aunt Kate Lovan about town, as if on a sightseeing tour.

Her voice had a monotone nasality. Anyone who had her as a typing teacher will recognize this refrain: "R, J, semi, space; R, J, semi, space;" which she called out to the class, smooth and connected, with the cadence of a metronome. In response, the class, in unison, pecked out the letters.

"R, J, semi, space" was followed by "O-L, O-L, O-L—I'm not saying what it sounds like I'm saying." Frankly, I was never quite sure what it was she thought she sounded like, but nevertheless, we reflexively typed the letters, and the cacophony of our pecking echoed in the wooden hallways outside.

According to her fellow teacher, Jessie Munford, she was without a peer as a proofreader. She could spot a typographical error with a glance. Mrs. Munford used to prevail upon her to review the *Willamizzou* for errors.

She could be perplexing, however. After I had gotten A's and B's on all the typing tests, I was surprised to see a D on my report card. I asked her why she gave me the low grade, and she said, "Anybody who slams his typewriter carriage, doesn't deserve a very good grade."

For younger readers, a typewriter is an old-fashioned, non-electric writing machine with a keyboard. The carriage is the moving part of the machine that supports a sheet of paper, which has to be manually moved by a lever, after each line of printing to advance to the next line.

For the record, I did not slam my typewriter carriage. It was a freshman boy who sat next to me, who shall remain anonymous. My pleas of innocence to Miss Masnor fell on deaf ears. It was obvious I needed to appeal to a higher authority. I reported the injustice to the principal, Fred Thomas, and he said he would take care of it. I don't know what he did, but my grade changed from a D to a B.

After that misunderstanding, I cruised through high school with no more D's, and arrived on the Mizzou campus in the fall of 1965 thinking I was a pretty good student. That is, until Professor Freeman posted grades for the Principles of Geology first mid-term exam.

Out of 25 seemingly easy multiple-choice questions, I had only gotten 16 correct, and the lowest C was 18. The class average for 400 students was 15—nearly half the class had D's and F's. I was from the Ozarks, and a class about rocks ought to be easy, but I had D.

That day in class, the professor seemed unphased by student protests about the exam. In response to one student's complaint that a question was unfair, he responded, "That's third-grade trigonometry." It may have been an obtuse response, but raised hands dropped and the questions stopped.

I still harbored the notion I was a good student and remained optimistic. After all, it was only the first of three exams, and I was doing OK in my other classes. I vowed to study harder.

A few weeks later, the grades on the second mid-term exam were posted. Again, for 25 multiple-choice questions, the lowest

C was 18, the class average was 15, and I got a 16—another D. Moreover, a pink deficiency slip was sent home to my parents advising them that their "scholar" was not making the grade.

My explanation to Mom that the pink slip was no big deal because half the class got them may have been a hint of my lawyering future, namely, telling the truth in the most favorable light. But the glibness of my explanation did not match the sinking feeling I felt. I only had one more mid-term before the final.

Hearing about my plight, a graduate student who ate in my dining hall, claimed that with hypnosis he could remove any anxiety I had concerning geology tests, which would free my mind to think more clearly. In desperation, I decided to get hypnotized before the next test.

In actual fact, I never felt hypnotized during the session, but the proof would lie in the results on the next test. The grades were posted. As usual, the lowest C was 18, the class average was 15, but I got a 17—still a D—but I had improved by a point. In spite of the improvement, I did not try hypnosis again.

The only thing between me and five hours of D in my first college semester was a fully-comprehensive 50-question final exam. It seemed hopeless.

During finals week, I discovered an unoccupied floor of my dormitory and hid there with a coffeepot and my geology book and notes. Time became a blur until the day of reckoning, and I stared at fifty seemingly easy multiple-choice questions.

Several days later, I trudged up to the final exam results taped on the lecture hall door anticipating another rebuke. I started reading from the bottom, through the F's, D's, C's, and I didn't see my student number in those groups. I looked again, but still didn't see it. I wasn't in the B's either. Finally, I started at the top. The highest score was 49, the second-highest was a 48—next to my student number. I had gotten an A on the fully comprehensive final . . . but still only received a C for the course. That hardly seemed fair, but I guess that was third-grade trigonometry.

My career includes seven years of college teaching, and to my students' chagrin, I always gave comprehensive finals. But, to show my enlightenment, I told them if they "aced" the final, they would get more than a C for the course. So there, Professor Freeman.

Today, I can't exactly remember what a reverse asymmetrical syncline is from the Principles of Geology class, nor have I had any need for the information. But thanks to Miss Masnor, "R, J, semi, space" from her typing class at WSHS still serves me well.

Wendell's 1982 Campaign and
the Pleasant Hill Chili Supper

IT HARDLY SEEMS POSSIBLE, but forty years ago this week during Wendell Bailey's 1980 U.S. Congressional campaign, I appeared on his behalf at the St. Louis County Pachyderms. Wendell had been invited to their "Meet the Candidates" event, but had to be in Willow Springs for a birthday party.

With a milestone birthday later this week, a bit of reflection about Wendell's storied career is fitting. After a stint as mayor of Willow Springs, he served four consecutive terms, 1972–1980, as a Missouri State Representative; in 1980 he became a U.S. Congressman; in 1984 he was elected Missouri Treasurer and was re-elected in 1988; and in 2000 he won the Republican nomination for Missouri Lieutenant Governor. Underscoring it all, he is a product of WSHS, Class of 1958.

For me, the most memorable Wendell Bailey campaign was the 1982 U.S. Congressional race. One of the highlights included Wendell and Jane Bailey on stage with Vice President

George H.W. Bush and Mrs. Bush at a packed auditorium in Blue Springs. Earlier that same evening, volunteers got to meet and shake hands with the vice president at a private function. After the rally, I answered the phone in the headquarters, and the call came from Air Force Two, the vice president's plane. In a moment, I was connected to Wendell who was flying back to DC.

But the 1982 campaign has a backstory. Wendell's Congressional story began two years earlier in the 1980 Republican primary in the old Missouri 8th District, when he bested 12 opponents running for the seat Richard Ichord (D–Houston) held for 19 years. In the general election, he beat Steve Gardiner (D–Ballwin), and distinguished himself as a freshman U.S. Congressman by actually passing legislation.

In 1980, Missouri's 8th District covered a large portion of central Missouri, from the Arkansas border, around the Lake of the Ozarks to Columbia, eastward along the Interstate 70 corridor to West St. Louis County, and southward through Dent, Shannon, and Oregon Counties.

In 1981, because of relatively low population growth in the 1970s, Missouri lost one of its ten Congressional districts. The redistricting process, courtesy of a Federal Court three–judge panel, dismantled the old 8th district by merging its eastern counties into the 10th District that was held by another Republican, Bill Emerson. The western counties became part of the 4th District, held by Democrat Ike Skelton.

As Ozarkers might say, that put Wendell between a rock and a hard place. The *New York Times* reported in February 1982 that "White House officials and other national party leaders have been urging Representative Wendell Bailey, who is being squeezed out of office by redistricting, to run against a Democratic incumbent, Representative Ike Skelton."

Lonnie Whitaker (L) and U.S. Congressman Wendell Bailey (R) greeting a local resident at a campaign chili supper in Pleasant Hill, Missouri. *The photo was originally published in the Pleasant Hill Times in October 1982.*

From a Republican national strategy, a chance to take down an incumbent democrat might have made sense, but it created numerous challenges for Wendell. The *New York Times* noted in the previous article that running against Ike Skelton meant "Mr. Bailey would probably establish a new residence, since his home in Willow Springs lies three and a half miles outside the new Fourth District. Forty percent of the residents of the new Fourth used to be in Mr. Bailey's old Eighth District in the south-central part of the state."

Wendell took the honorable high road and refused to run against a fellow Republican. Instead, he took on the formidable challenge of running, essentially, outside of his old district against a popular incumbent Democrat congressman and former state senator, who retained 60% of his district after the remapping.

Wendell offered me an opportunity to work on the 1982 Congressional race, and I arrived at the headquarters in Blue Springs one afternoon in June. Wasting no time, campaign manager Duane Benton (now a judge for the U.S. Court of Appeals for the Eighth Circuit) gave me the keys to a Pontiac, loaded it with Bailey for Congress yard signs, and dispatched me to Pleasant Hill in Cass County.

Pleasant Hill and the surrounding counties became my area to establish a beachhead in "enemy" territory. I trudged the streets, knocked on doors, hawked campaign material, and made a daily stop at the office of the *Pleasant Hill Times* to chat with the editor, who said he was impressed with my enthusiasm.

Progress in Pleasant Hill was steady but unremarkable, and Wendell decided we needed to hold an event there. Since I had been selected to be a judge in the Missouri Chili Cookoff, and imagined myself to be a "chili head," I suggested we hold a chili supper. Wendell said, "Okay, do it." Suddenly, I got a sinking feeling as I imagined the size of the task and the possibility for failure. One of Wendell's catchphrases was "lack of blame is sufficient reward." I could see blame on the horizon. Why did I open my big mouth?

I reserved a date at the Pleasant Hill Memorial Building, a venue that had dining capacity and a kitchen with a stove, refrigerator, and cooking utensils. I ordered a half-gallon of chili powder from a spice company, and purchased the remaining food items and paper products from a small grocery store in Pleasant

Hill. The store was owned by a young couple who allowed me to display a Bailey sign in their window.

With the logistics in place, all I needed was assistance from some of the staffers. At a staff party the night before the chili supper, several people promised to help, but the next morning nobody showed. We had advertised the free chili event and anticipated a crowd, and now the responsibility was on my shoulders.

I hightailed it to Pleasant Hill where I had a trunk load of groceries, including 40 pounds of ground beef, waiting to be picked up.

Inside the store, I chatted with the proprietors as I paid for the supplies. An owner's mother, a gray-haired lady who always sat quietly on a stool behind the counter, asked how many were helping me. I explained the situation to her and then asked, "Grandma, do you know anything about making chili?" She said, "No . . . but I'll help you."

I loaded the groceries into the car, and with Grandma riding shotgun, headed to the Memorial Building. By now, it was past noon, and time was of the essence. Fortunately, the kitchen had 4 5-gallon cooking pots. I put 10 pounds of ground beef in each one and started browning the meat. Grandma sorted the onions, garlic, and peppers, and opened bean and tomato cans. By 2 p.m., we had 4 pots of "Texas Red" simmering.

That evening we served approximately 100 people. My visits to the newspaper office may have paid dividends because the event was covered by the *Pleasant Hill Times*, with a front-page photo. An explanation about the photo is in order. The apron I was wearing came from the Missouri Chili Cookoff, which was sponsored by Budweiser. Just before the photo was snapped, I pasted a Wendell Bailey bumper sticker over the "King of Beers" logo.

Although the '82 race didn't have the result we had hoped for, the effort was significant in two respects: the two-term incumbent Democrat was held to 54% of the vote, and Wendell's state-wide recognition expanded, which helped his comeback as state treasurer two years later.

I'll conclude with an apt quote from Theodore Roosevelt: "It is not the critic who counts; not the man who points out how the strong man stumbles; or where the doer of deeds could have done them better. The credit belongs to the man who is actually in the arena . . . ." And Wendell has certainly been in the arena. Happy Birthday to my friend and mentor, and Willow's favorite son.

Origin of an Ozark Novel

IF YOU ARE A writer, whether you're John-Boy Walton of the TV series, *The Waltons*, or Tobias Wolf, author of the bestselling memoir, *This Boy's Life*, your family and where you grew up provide a wealth of writing material.

It's true for me growing up in the Ozarks. I still recall the images—almost like color photographs in my mind—and remember the aromas and the feelings with clarity. Often, the memories are common place and personal, such as the day in 1958 I rode with mill-worker and farmer, Johnny McVicker, in his Chevy pickup truck to the crossroads store in Montier. Why I remember it, I haven't a clue, and I only recall riding with him one time.

In my mind's eye, I can still see Johnny in bib overalls, a chambray work shirt, and well-worn high-top shoes, and in need of a shave. The smell of sweat and tobacco, from an ever-present cigarette hanging from his mouth, permeated the truck, even with both windows down on a sunny summer day. The floorboard of the truck, littered with loose tools and a

Sinclair oil can, rattled when he shifted gears. I replicated this scene in my novel *Geese to a Poor Market*, albeit with the setting in Texas and a Mexican character named José.

One of my favorite characters in my novel is Ethan Collier, whom I often describe as a combination of Ernest T. Bass, the rock-chucking hillbilly with no social skills from *The Andy Griffith Show*, and Raymond Babbitt, the autistic savant played by Dustin Hoffman in the 1988 movie *Rain Man.* Really, the character Ethan is a combination of traits from two actual people, one from Montier and the other from Willow Springs.

In the 1950s, a hermit named Billy Barnes lived near Montier across the gravel road from my grandparents in a shack made from rough-sawn boards, with cracks chinked with newspaper. It might be better described as a toolshed.

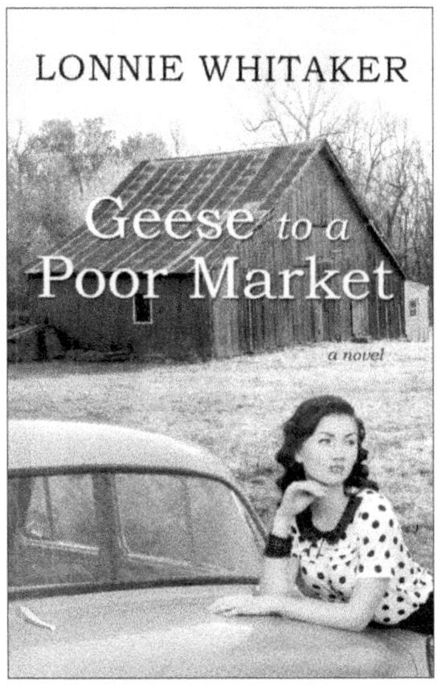

Lonnie Whitaker's debut novel, *Geese to a Poor Market*, a geographic slice of Americana, with an ensemble cast of crooks, moonshiners, preachers, and lawyers that has one leg that wants to boogie and other planted on a pew.

Inside, various implements of labor—hoes, shovels, rakes, a scythe—hung on the walls.

He had a small heating stove, which also served as a cookstove. Once, Grandpa got Billy to help him dig potatoes in our garden, and for his help, gave him a half-bushel of spuds. When

Billy cooked them, he dumped the potatoes, dirt and all, in a pot and boiled them. I do not know if he had electricity, but his water came from a rock-walled cistern that was frequently home to ring-necked snakes. That cistern and the snakes show up in a scene at Ethan's place.

Billy didn't own a car, and I regularly saw him crouched forward, traipsing with an odd gait on his way to the country store a mile away. His appearance never changed: gray hair poked out over his ears and shirt collar from underneath a soiled railroad cap. His dirt-stained overalls always looked stiff from lack of washing.

Most people didn't pay much attention to Billy, and some shied away from him—I didn't because I took a plate of dinner to him every Sunday afternoon. All he said when I delivered the meal, and the only thing I remember him ever saying, was, "Much obliged."

According to my grandmother, Billy wasn't always a recluse. In fact, 40 years before he had been a dapper young man in the country community. With some admiration in her voice, she said he always wore a starched shirt. Billy had been engaged to be married, and showed up at the church, but his fiancé didn't. And Billy was never the same afterwards.

The other dimension of Ethan was inspired by William Rothwell, one of eleven children of Howell County residents George and Mamie Rothwell, and my stepfather's youngest brother.

I never met William, or Bill as he was known, but I heard stories from my stepfather about his brother's remarkable mental abilities. He told me Bill could stand at the old railroad depot in Willow Springs and recite the names of all the boxcars of the trains after they passed through.

Perhaps, some of the stories about Bill are "urban legends," but the 1939 *Willamizzou* quipped, "He's got a memory, but he needs a girl." One story, which I've heard from several sources, involves the police going to him after a local physician had been kidnapped in January 1937, to ask if he had seen any strange cars in town. He had supposedly committed most of the license plates in Willow to memory. As the story goes, he provided information, including license plate numbers, that was instrumental in capturing the perpetrators.

In a writers' workshop I attended in the course of writing the novel, several women members insisted that I make a romantic connection between Ethan and another character, an attractive former cheerleader. I protested that it was unrealistic, but I finally agreed to try. As a result, Bill and Billy got another shot at romance in a chapter called Ethan and the Marquess of Queensbury.

A novel by definition is fictional and not autobiographical. Tobias Wolf in a 2003 interview for *The Missouri Review*, explained how the lines may blur. "I might use colors from the same palette and use experiences from my memory and my own life, but I take off. I'm not loyal to the facts or my own memory. I'm really inventing."

In my experience, and I've heard it from other writers, too, if an actual event is included in fictional writing, that's the part nobody believes. A writing instructor told me, "Just because something happened doesn't mean it's believable."

People are sometimes curious about the meaning of the title, *Geese to a Poor Market*. It's a saying I heard as a child, but I understand it may have originated in England and reached the Ozarks by way of Appalachia. Essentially, it means selling yourself or your goods for less than value. If a girl was marrying some rascal, folks would say, "She's driving her geese to a poor market." Similarly, I'd hear it from my parents if I was hanging out with the "wrong crowd." As to the characters in the book, it relates to the choices they make.

As the late radio personality Paul Harvey might say, "Now, you know the rest of the story."

Salamander Summer

IF I HAVE ANY patience at all, it results from having lived with my grandmother, Beulah McKillip Casey, during my formative years as a child on a Shannon County farm.

Grandma was born in 1899 to Civil War veteran Alexander McKillip, who by all accounts was a mild-mannered man, and his wife Della, who, by many accounts, possessed a flinty disposition. Great grandma Della once killed a man with a pitchfork in defense of her husband, who was being beaten up by some ruffian. In her later years, when I was a baby, she threatened to stab a photographer who had the gall to say, "that baby isn't photogenic." She had apparently mellowed with age, defending her darling great grandchild.

Great grandma Della, smoked a clay pipe and was supposedly one-quarter Native American, but given recent news coverage concerning family histories, I don't state that as a fact. She had husbands other than Alexander. One came home drunk, and she sewed him in the bedsheets while he was passed out and thrashed him with a bed slat. The legal pleading might have read, "plaintiff was bruised, contused, and made sore and painful."

Speaking of punishment, she bought buggy whips for Grandma and her sister Fern at the county fair, which she promptly took from them once they got home, and strategically placed them over doorways to use as switches on the girls.

These snapshots of Della are just a sampling, but provide sufficient evidence to suggest her nature and my grandmother's perseverance.

Thanks goodness, Grandma didn't take after her mother. Surprisingly, I don't recall Grandma ever expressing strong resentments of Della, other than once saying, "she was a mean old rip." That's amazing since Della also put Grandma and Fern in an orphanage after their father died. I have a sad postcard that Aunt Fern sent her mom from the orphanage.

Perhaps, by the time I came along, after Grandma had endured a volatile mother, the 1918 Spanish Flu Pandemic, the Great Depression, two stillborn babies, her husband's arm amputation, and two World Wars, she took the heat of Ozark summers in the 1950s without breaking her stride.

Just a toe-raise over five feet tall and stoutly built, Grandma worked hard with little complaint. During the day, she helped her one-armed husband with outside chores, and still found the energy to can tomatoes over a woodburning cookstove at 2 a.m. to avoid the heat.

Living in the un-airconditioned farmhouse, I remember those hot summers well. The uninsulated attic where my brother and I slept, which was as dry and hot as a sauna, had to be abandoned for army cots on the first floor. A window fan in the living room offered little relief.

Quoting Pat Guinan, associate professor of climatology with the University of Missouri Extension, the October 2013 *Agricultural Electronic Bulletin Board* reported that 1954 ranked as the third hottest summer on record. Moreover, ". . . between 1952 and 1956 southwest Missouri accumulated a deficit of 60 inches of precipitation."

This created a problem for our Shannon County farm. By 1957, the cistern ran out of water. We actually had a well, but it hadn't been functional for years, and with no funds to fix it, the cistern was our only source of water.

Our cistern was basically a cylindrical-shaped hole in the ground that collected rain water from gutter downspouts on the house. Constructed of concrete and about 10 feet deep and 8 feet wide, it could hold over 3,000 gallons. A rectangular wooden cabinet, with a hinged lid and an overhead pulley hoist and scaffold, covered the 3-by 3-foot opening. To get water, a rope and bucket attached to the overhead pulley took the place of a pump.

Grandpa arranged for a tanker truck that held 2,000 gallons to deliver water from Mountain View. But first the cistern needed to be cleaned. After most of the remaining water had been bailed out, there still remained a layer of mud at the bottom that had to be swabbed. Grandpa was too old to attempt going down, so I got the assignment.

With one foot in the bucket and holding on to the pulley rope, my skinny 10-year-old self, stripped down to my Fruit of the Loom skivvies, was lowered into the abyss. To this day, I vividly remember the feeling of stepping out of the bucket. It felt as if I had stepped into six inches of chocolate pudding. Dust filtering in over the years had formed a layer of slimy mud.

It was dark and creepy at the bottom of the cistern, but it wasn't the damp and darkness that concerned me. Four feet away at the edge of the cistern floor, two large cave salamanders eyed me. One, orange with black spots, and the other yellow with black spots. *Eurycea lucifuga.*

Now, this concerned me.

Grandma kept a salamander in a fishbowl in the living room as a pet. She called it a "waterdog" and cautioned me to stay away from it because waterdogs were poisonous. Her puny, grayish waterdog was only three inches, head to tail, compared to the plump six-inch monsters staring at me.

In my mind they had to be first cousins to Gila monsters. It didn't help that my brother Jack, who was four years older, and too big to be let down by the pulley, taunted me that those lizards could jump several feet.

As an adult, I always laughed that grandma had said they were poisonous. Researching this article, however, I was surprised to discover she was right. According to the Missouri Department of Conservation, salamanders secrete a neurotoxin if handled. I wonder where she got this, yet, another example of her country wisdom.

With her usual patience, Grandma assured me that the waterdogs wouldn't bother me if I left them alone, and I began dipping the bucket into the mud, while keeping an eye on the salamanders. When most of the mud was scooped up, she threw down some tow sacks (burlap feed sacks) to mop up the bottom.

As a side note, I have often been curious why my grandparents called burlap bags tow sacks. With a little online investigation, I discovered it's because they are made out of "tow," which are waste fibers not suitable for better cloth. Another factoid: Chicken feed, on the other hand, came in more proper cloth, including colorful prints. I know because Grandma made a yellow shirt for me, from a chicken pellet sack, on her old Singer foot pedal-operated sewing machine.

By the way, the salamanders were not removed prior to refilling the cistern, and I don't think Great Grandma Della would have been afraid of them. She would have been searching for a fish gig.

Riley and Beulah Casey's Shannon County farmhouse near Montier, Missouri, circa 1955. The women are Opal Whitaker (L) and her best friend, Frances Mizer.

Two Decades of Football in Willow—Part 1

THE CURRENT NEWS CONCERNING whether football will be played in colleges this fall got me to thinking about football in Willow Springs back in my day—the Fifties and Sixties. During those decades, I knew all the coaches, and either played for them or had them as teachers.

The boys who suited up will remember those hot days of August, a couple weeks before school started, when two-a-day football practices began. In the mornings, before the heat became stifling, players assembled on the dusty practice field behind what is now Munford Gym. The second round happened in the evenings under the lights at Palenske Field. And each year practice commenced with high hopes for a better season than the last.

Back then, coaches had this misguided idea if players drank water during practice, they might get upset stomachs. All I remember is being parched and gulping water like a horse when practice was over. During practice, my mind would nearly hallucinate with visions of ice-cold watermelons or frosty mugs of root beer from the A&W. Now, in the age of enlightenment and Gatorade, withholding water would be considered cruel and usual punishment and the basis for litigation.

When I moved to Willow in 1959, the quality of Willow football teams was dismal. Folks reminisced about the good ol' days when Coach Harold "Speedo" Harmon's teams won South Central Association (SCA) conference championships in 1950, 1951 and 1952.

Speedo's teams won 33 straight games and notched two consecutive victories in the post-season Ozark Bowl played in the Southwest Missouri State College (SMS) stadium in Springfield. The Bears beat Lockwood (12–6) and Eldorado Springs (19–9) in 1950 and 1951.

Dean Belshe (WSHS, '56) who attended each Ozark Bowl game, says, "Many of us took the train to Springfield. It seemed like most of the town at the time." According to the 1951 *Willa-mizzou*, "Businesses closed down in Willow Springs; the Bear Boosters charted a special train; and the marching band and drum corps gave their instruments an extra polish." Personally, I recall admiring the large Ozark Bowl trophy enshrined in the trophy case of the old high school building.

The Bears also beat Springfield Central in a postseason game in 1952 after their third sweep of the SCA. Cheerleader Helen Benton (Birdsong) (WSHS, '53) wore her cheerleading sweater into a local drive-in after the Springfield game and says, "There was complete silence when they saw my cheerleading sweater— we didn't stay long."

Ace running back Sonny Stringer garnered all-state honorable mention in 1951. In 1952, he received first-team all-state recognition, and that same year, passed for a record-setting 353 yards against Springfield Central and rushed for four touchdowns against Rolla. After graduation, his legend as a running back continued at the University of Missouri. I met Sonny a few years ago at a Memorial Day reunion, and he looked like he could still run pretty fast.

By the end of the fifties, however, the glory days of football in Willow had faded, but hope arose with the arrival of Ben Koeneman in 1959. Coach Koeneman, a Mount Vernon, Missouri, native was an all-league lineman from SMS, and a man with a soft-spoken, serious demeanor.

Coach Harold "Speedo" Harmon and the 1950 WSHS Bear "bantam weight" backfield of an undefeated team that won the SCA Conference and the Ozark Bowl. Sonny "Buck" Stringer (20), Junior Christopher (22), Neil Hanks (31), and Bill Flood (24). *Photo is from the 1951 Willamizzou.*

Although he had spent two years in the service before returning for his senior year at SMS, his solemn bearing apparently came naturally. Retired Mount Vernon judge, Sam Jones, told me that while in grade school he and a buddy were hitchhiking when then high school star Ben Koeneman picked them up to caution them about the dangers of hitchhiking. Once, during my eighth-grade year, he admonished me about eating pastries on game day when he saw me eating a donut—and he wasn't even my coach. When he signed my yearbook, he checked a dictionary to make sure he spelled athlete correctly. The word still bears the corrective smudge.

After 34 years of the single-wing offense in Willow, Coach Koeneman introduced the modern split-T formation. John Tandy, a senior that year, says, "We had to work hard to switch from the single-wing to the T." John also recalls another transition he had to make. "I had to take off my football gear and switch to a band uniform for the halftime music show."

With the new offensive scheme, on October 23, 1959, the Bears won their first game in two years beating the Houston Tigers 21–7—the only win for the season. Coach Koeneman left after two years to coach at Salem.

For the 1961 season, junior high coach, Buddy Bennett, received a promotion to head high school football coach. I remember watching another poor season from the bench my freshman year. Plagued by injuries, the team only managed a record of one win, three ties, and six losses. Apparently, his three-a-day preseason practices didn't help. Coach Bennett transferred to coach at Buffalo the next year.

Coach Robert E. Lee arrived in 1962, with an impressive resume. After a distinguished career at Mizzou, he played professionally with the New England Patriots and the Calgary Stampeders. Here's a bit of trivia I couldn't resist including. In high school, he won the Missouri state shot put championship in 1954, 40 years after his dad won the same title in 1914.

Unfortunately, Willow lost every game in 1962, except the last of the season, when we managed to beat Mountain View 20–13. I remember that game well because Coach Lee taped my injured knee so thoroughly, I practically hobbled around on the field. Coach Lee left after one year to coach at Kemper Military School in Booneville.

Two Decades of Football in Willow—Part 2

IN 1963, A CHANGING tide, or, maybe, a small hurricane rolled in with the arrival of tough-as-nails Joel Case. Coach Case, another Mizzou football letterman, had a swagger that he imparted to the team. Fans started coming to the games again. My mom said part of the reason for the increased attendance was that folks wanted to watch Coach Case on the sidelines. He'd charge up and down the field, yell at the refs, and occasionally throw his clipboard.

In practices, he was the most physically involved coach I remember. Donning a helmet snatched from a player, he would demonstrate blocking and tackling techniques. He seemed to love returning punts in practice. One time when he was receiving punts, I rushed around the line and charged toward him. Just before I launched in the air for a stupendous tackle, he pivoted toward me. I still remember the devilish grin on his face just before he straightened me up with a forearm shiver.

That wasn't the only time that year I received a comeuppance. During practice one day, Eddie Mack Hill connected with a short pass to me. I had made it past the linebackers, and the only defensive player between me and the goal line was one of the freshman on the team. I could have easily evaded him, but with upperclassman hubris, I decided to plow into him.

I can think of numerous clichés to describe the result, but suffice to say, it was a poor choice on my part. The freshman wrapped both arms around my legs, and I went down with a thump to a chorus of cheers from my teammates. I felt a bit embarrassed, but, for sure, the freshman impressed me that day.

We only won two games that year—both against Mountain View—but with Hill as quarterback, we led the conference in passing. Moreover, several players received SCA honors: Dan Holloway, first team, and Jim Kilpatrick, Bill Tandy, Truman Grogan, Ed Hill, Lonnie Whitaker, and Dan Zimmerman received honorable mention.

Coach Case, to the team's disappointment, only stayed for one season. He left for law school. To his credit, he has come to most of my class's reunions and appears to have retained his athletic physique and never-back-down attitude.

In 1964, David Meek arrived as the fifth coach in five years, but he inherited 19 returning letterman, and a senior class (of '65) that had played together since junior high. With a defensive orientation, he brought balance to a team that had shown they could score against anybody the previous year.

The 1964 team took second place in the SCA with a 7-1 conference record, losing only to Cabool. The loss was a 13-7 heartbreaker, with a pass interference call against the Bulldogs in the waning minutes that prevented a nearly certain winning touchdown and a share of the conference championship. To this day, I remember the name of the Cabool player who committed the foul and the spot on Palenske Field where the infraction occurred. For many of us on the team that year, that game is a melancholy "what if" memory that has lasted a lifetime.

In SCA awards, Lynn Jones and Lonnie Whitaker, received first-team honors; Dan Zimmerman was tapped for the second team backfield; and Ed Hill, Tom Siegrist, Jim Johnson, Jody Corn, and Terry Collins received honorable mention. Whitaker also received honorable mention to the All-Ozark squad.

Finally, a conference championship—the first in 13 years. In the 1966 season, under the guidance of Coach Meek, the Bears compiled an 8-2 record to become co-champions with Mountain Grove. John Twist, in addition to being first-team all-confer-ence, received first-team

From the WSHS 196 team, Lonnie Whitaker (81) and Lynn Jones (73), both first-team SCA, watch Dan Zimmerman (10), second-team SCA, help his little brother Jay into his home jersey. *Photo is from the 1965 Willamizzou.*

all-Ozark and all-state honorable mention. Coach Meek was named SCA coach of the year. Other Bears received SCA honors in 1966: Jim Gooch, first team fullback; Steve Foster, first team center; Steve Koch, first team end; Randy James, first team linebacker; Steve Steele, second team halfback; Lyndel Brown, second team tackle; Don Pigg, honorable mention quarterback; "Punkie" Stevenson, honorable mention guard; and "Buster" Graves, honorable mention guard.

Steve Foster, a senior on the championship team, says, "Our team was far from explosive offensively, but the defense was rugged and stingy." Willow finished 7th in the conference in scoring, but first in defense. The defense was anchored by SCA Lineman of the Year, John Twist, and all-conference first-team linebacker, Randy James. "Twist was big, strong and quick as a cat. James was a very aggressive and physical linebacker who could cleanup any play the lineman didn't," says Foster.

Although Willow beat Mountain Grove that year, the Bears had a remorseful loss on a hot Saturday afternoon late in the season to arch rival West Plains. Foster says, "We only had 18 team members and played only 11 or 12 players. I think the heat and WP's depth took its toll on the Bears. That loss still haunts me because I think we had the best team."

The Bears didn't win another championship that decade, but I would be remiss if I didn't mention the impressive accomplishments of Bill Gooch who was named to the All-Ozark 2nd team backfield in 1968 and 1969, and received All-State Honorable Mention in 1969.

From Sonny Stringer to John Twist and Bill Gooch, and the years in between, the skirmishes under the Friday night lights of Palenske Field forged memories for the boys who wore the maroon jerseys, the fans in the stands, and the cheerleaders on the sidelines. Memories of thrilling victories still bragged about; losses to West Plains and Cabool that still haunt; Truman Grogan's 90-yard kickoff return for a TD against West Plains;

a tackle that prompted Neil Hanks to buy me a steak dinner; pretty homecoming queens; and images of cheerleaders on chilly nights wearing borrowed letter jackets and shaking maroon and white pompoms and yelling for the Bears. Memories, of the way we were.

And speaking of cheerleaders, my thanks to Alice Brook (WSHS '67) and Sadie Burns (WSHS '68) for photographs. Go Bears!

More Tales From Country School Days

LIKE SHERLOCK HOLMES, THE fictional English detective, I have an older, smarter brother. Jack will admit he is four years older but deny that he is smarter. Nevertheless, my observation is true. Generally, this has proved to be a blessing, but at times during my childhood, I would have cringed at such a notion.

Consider the "Case of the Vanishing Cupcake." My grandmother was a wonderful cook. I still recall the smell of homemade bread baking in the woodburning cookstove. Bread, which would be topped with butter, churned from the milk of our Jersey cow. But my favorite of her baked wonders were cupcakes—and my brother knew this.

One afternoon in our back yard, when Jack saw me staring at the freshly-baked cupcake in his hand, he lifted it to his nose, inhaled audibly, and said, "Hmmm, this smells good." He had my rapt attention. "Let me have a bite," I pleaded. With both hands, he clutched the cupcake to his chest as if he were protecting a baby chick from a predator. "No," he said, "you'll eat the whole thing." I promised to only take a nibble. "Okay, then, just a tiny bite," he said, and handed me the cupcake.

With the gusto of a hound dog, I crammed half of the cupcake into my mouth. Before my brain could inform me that something was wrong, I started gagging and coughing. My stomach convulsed and my eyes watered, as I tried to spit out the cupcake. He had filled it with red and black pepper. I don't recall if he got in trouble for his shenanigan, but I suspect Grandma only mildly admonished him. But then, he was always her favorite. Harrumph.

And then there was the case of "The Mysterious Card Trick," when I was a gullible 9-year-old. With TV generally unavailable at the old Shannon County farmhouse, Jack and I often played card games with our grandparents. The usual game was Pitch, but Jack and I also played a game called "Drink or Smell," which we learned from an old cowboy movie—but that's another story. The point is, we were always fooling around with a deck of cards.

Somewhere, Jack had learned a card trick. After shuffling the cards, he'd fan them on the table and have me select a card, and without showing it to him, return it to the deck. After apparently reshuffling, he would identify the card I had picked. I pleaded with him to tell me the secret to the trick, but he refused to tell me.

Finally, after persistent begging (and probably after promising to do some of his chores) he said, "The secret to the trick is you smell the cards." Even as naïve as I was, I was skeptical and accused him of fibbing. But with pokerfaced righteousness, he assured me he was telling the truth. To prove his point, he raised the Ace of Spades to his nose and sniffed at it. "The aces smell like gravy," he said, and handed it to me to smell.

My brother, like any conman worth his salt, knew that a victim's downfall hinges on the desire for the gimmick to be true. I took the ace from him and, by golly, I thought the card did smell a little bit like gravy. Then he told me the kings smelled like oranges, and that all I needed to do was practice. And somehow, the trick seemed to work when Jack picked the card.

[Note to readers: At this point, I have abandoned any attempt to edit the story so I don't look like a complete nitwit.]

I practiced, sniffing and shuffling, until I was beginning to believe the trick actually worked, and could hardly wait to show off for my buddies at the Montier school. The next day, I hid the cards in my pocket and smuggled them onto the school bus. I figured I had to be sneaky because one boy had gotten a whipping for bringing chewing tobacco to school, and I imagined a deck of cards might be a worse infraction.

The schoolhouse at Montier, based on old photographs and correspondence I have, was built before 1920. The interior of the white clapboard structure, behind the kitchen and cloakroom at the front, had a large central area divided into two classrooms by a heavy wooden folding door. On one side, which was referred to as the "Little Room," Mrs. Margaret Shockley taught grades one through four. On the other side, her husband Wilbert taught grades five through eight in the "Big Room." My brother was an eighth-grader in the Big Room.

That morning before recess, and my opportunity to demonstrate the trick, a student from the Big Room came over and told

Mrs. Shockley that Mr. Shockley wanted to see me. My mind went to full-alert status. "Did he say why?" Mrs. Shockley asked. The student indicated that he hadn't.

I proceeded to the Big Room, and all four rows of students—each row a separate grade—watched as I entered. Mr. Shockley motioned me to his desk and said, "I understand you know a card trick." With some hesitance, I told him that I did. "What's the secret to it?" he asked. An anxious feeling hit my stomach, and, no doubt, with a tentative voice, I told him that it involved smelling the cards. At that point, all four grades broke into uproarious laughter.

Needless to say, at that moment I wanted to crawl inside a hole and disappear, but a sudden awareness struck me: the real secret of the trick was that I had been tricked. The fortunate thing about childhood attention spans is they are short lived. At recess, some of my buddies laughed, others expressed sympathy, but after lunch I don't recall the matter ever being mentioned again.

It is unlikely that latter day teachers, including me, would set up a student for public embarrassment. But surprisingly, that incident never sparked a resentment of Mr. Shockley. He teased everyone, and I still consider him one of the best teachers I ever had. However, the "Case of the Purloined Note," which I will save for another day, did get my dander up.

But there are blessings from the cases of the "Vanishing Cupcake" and "The Mysterious Card Trick." If I am ever accused of being a suspicious, cynical curmudgeon, I can blame it on my brother.

Election Memories and the Student Council

WITH POLITICS IN THE air, I recall that casting my first vote in a U.S. presidential election in 1960 created a dilemma for me. Who should get my vote?" Two-term Vice President Richard M. Nixon or the dashing challenger, John F. Kennedy.

Wait a second . . . he's not that old, you might be thinking, and you would be right. But when I was in the 8th grade, the WSHS Student Council sponsored a mock election that included junior high students.

Deanna (Collins) Corn, a freshman that year, says, "I do remember the mock election. It was very exciting . . . before we had 24/7 cable news." But we had TV, with The Huntley–Brinkley Report ("Good Night, Chet." "Good night, David"), and the election had generated considerable excitement, even with students.

The Nixon/Kennedy contest wasn't the first mock presidential election held at the high school. I can't address earlier years, but on November 4, 1952, Myrtle Dunivin, after training her American government students in the election process, conducted a mock election. Her government students explained balloting procedures to students and then served as election officials.

In 1952, students chose Republican Dwight Eisenhower, who won the national election, over Democrat Adlai Stevenson, but followed the state trend and chose Democrat Phil Donnelly over Republican Howard Elliott for governor. Howell County voters went Republican for both president and governor. Shannon County went Democratic for both.

Political trivia: Donnelly and Christopher Bond are the only Missouri governors to serve two non-consecutive terms.

I can't say for sure who sponsored a mock election for the 1956 replay between President Eisenhower and Adlai Stevenson, but according to the 1960 *Willamizzou*, the Student Council was only in its third year in the 1959-1960 school year. Regardless, the 1956 election is interesting to me for several reasons, and is the backdrop to a sidebar story.

Although Ike won in a landslide, Missouri was one of only seven states that went Democratic that year. But it was a close call in Missouri—Stevenson edged Ike by less than 4,000 votes statewide, because of a 72,000-vote advantage in the City of St. Louis. Howell County went Republican with 64% of the votes, but Shannon County went Democratic, with 60% of the votes.

Living in Shannon County in 1956 resulted in an unfortunate situation for my grandfather. In today's political climate, folks are often hesitant to reveal the candidate of their choice out of fear of being shunned and avoided or held up to contempt and ridicule. Maybe it is worse today, but it's not a new dynamic.

My grandparents generally stuck with the philosophy of not talking about religion or politics. Both would say they voted for the man and not the party, however, a color portrait of Ike and Mamie Eisenhower, which my grandmother had cut from the cover of a magazine, hung in a frame over their bed. Mamie in a vibrant blue gown, and Ike in a handsome suit and tie.

Grandpa worked the night shift at the Pagett-Smith Flooring Mill in Mountain View. He carpooled with three other men from the Montier community, and parked his car at the Montier Grocery on old Highway 60.

One evening on the way to the mill, the subject of the presidential election came up. Grandpa, a plainspoken, generally quiet man, joined the conversation, and said, "I think Ike is a good man." The comment must have weighed heavily on the Shannon County Democrat who drove, to the extent it rendered Grandpa's companionship unbearable. The next night he informed Grandpa that he was no longer welcome to ride.

I recall that it hurt Grandpa's feelings because the man was his friend. It worried my grandmother that Grandpa would have to drive on the hilly curves of old Highway 60 at night, after working the late shift.

I'm still not altogether sure about Grandma's politics, but after she moved to Willow Springs in the Seventies, she voted for Wendell Bailey for the Missouri House, and defended his honor when an old lady across the street referred to him as a hippie. No doubt, the old lady had seen Grandma's Bailey sign in her front yard. But Wendell a hippie? Yeah, I laughed when I heard it, too.

The 1965 *Willamizzou* indicates the student council sponsored another mock election, which would have been the 1964 race between incumbent Lyndon Johnson and Senator Barry Goldwater of Arizona. However, the yearbook copy had no details, and unlike the 1960 mock election, I barely remember it—and I wrote the yearbook copy. Nationally, the race didn't generate much excitement either. LBJ carried 44 of 50 states, including Missouri.

What did generate excitement at WSHS, were the student council elections. Sandy Merrill and I were sophomore representatives in the 1962–63 school year when senior Brenda Burns and Mike Sears were president and vice president. The year before, Brenda had been vice president with senior president Bill Haas. In those races, some electioneering took place, with a few posters in the hallways, but mainly, the candidates made stump speeches at a school assembly.

The following year, however, campaigning skyrocketed when Deanna Collins and Pat Stringer ran against Bill Tandy and Mike Warning. Campaign signs covered the hallways, lockers, and bathrooms. Inside the cover of the 1963 *Willamizzou*, a two-page spread photo shows Tandy and Warning standing on the auditorium stage surrounded by ten posters.

And there were "personal" attacks. At the time, Dial soap was the leading deodorant soap in the country, with an advertising slogan: "Aren't you glad you use Dial: (Don't you wish everybody did?)" The Collins/Stringer duo used this popular catchphrase to suggest the Tandy/Warning team could benefit from using Dial soap.

Principal Fred Thomas and home economics teacher Ruth Mathieu expressed concern that the campaigns had become unseemly, although neither intervened. Undaunted, Tandy and Warning posted a large sign in response: "If Elected We Promise to Use Dial!!!! –Tandy and Warning." They won the election.

Notoriously competitive, the Class of '65 fielded three sets of candidates in the student council race our senior year: Annette Tetrick and Donna Spence, running with a "For Better Student Body Representation" slogan; Glenda Turner and Jim Thomas, with a T N T logo (Thomas and Turner); and Lonnie Whitaker and junior Bill Shanks, a popular student and outstanding basketball player. My classmates had better signage, but the result was determined by demographic strategy. The senior class split its votes, but Shanks and I got most of the junior class votes and won.

That year basketball coach Bob Martin was the student council advisor. He and I counted the votes for Hoop Queen, and sophomore Alice West won. The question arose who would kiss the queen at the halftime coronation. Traditionally, the honor went to the team captain, but Coach Martin, apparently wanting to keep the captain's mind focused on the game, suggested the student council president should do it. I don't recall that I had any hesitation breaking tradition, and as one former U.S. president said, "Elections have consequences."

Banjo Blues

I'VE BEEN ABSENT MINDED since birth. As a kid I was forever losing things—combs, watches, ball gloves—you name it. My hands had the ability to operate independently of any cerebral process, as if each had a mind of its own. I still wish I had the wristwatch I left in the dressing room at Smoky Stover's swimming pool in Willow in 1962.

My mind would center on something of interest while, unbeknownst to it, my hand would lay whatever it was holding in an obvious spot never to be found again. I understand why my Irish ancestors believed in those prankish wee folk—leprechauns and fairies, who sneak around and hide things.

Age has not improved my absent-mindedness. If anything, it has compounded the problem with age-related issues such as short-term memory impairment, "senior moments," and CRS (can't remember stuff).

So, after countless incidents of staring vacantly into the refrigerator because I couldn't remember why I had opened it, or going on scavenger hunts several times a week to find my car keys, I decided to take action before I was placed in a nursing home before my time. Because my brother ran the nursing home, and still remembers that as a toddler I wrecked his trove of toys, this could be another problem.

Articles abound in popular magazines and on the internet about the importance of exercising the senior mind to stay vital and engaged. The mind is like a muscle they say—use it or lose it. My wife's solution is Sudoku, that mind-boggling numbers grid invented by Swiss mathematician over 200 years ago and popularized more recently by a Japanese publisher. But that's too much like arithmetic for someone who got a "C" in college algebra. (In my defense, I overslept and missed most of a midterm exam.).

My mother-in-law, who maintained a sharp mind and disposing memory into her nineties, worked crossword puzzles all her life. Crossword puzzles are not for me. They involve too many obscure words like "ova" and esoteric names of Greek muses or the moons of Jupiter.

Then there's the old standard—learn a new language. Not for me, either. I'm fine with the two years of French I learned from Mr. Findley at WSHS—it sustained me for a summer in Europe. Plus, that would mean going to class at night. I spent seven years teaching evening classes at colleges, and I'm too old for that, now. And, as my wife will attest, my brain shuts down after 8:00 p.m.

I read someplace that learning to play a musical instrument was good for the developing brains of children, as well as the declining minds of seniors. Now, that seemed like a possibility. It sounded better than sitting in front of the courthouse whittling with the codgers I used to see on trips to West Plains. [My apologies to any current gentlemen woodcarvers.]

The piano was out of the question—entirely too intimidating. Then my aging mind, which still tries to engage in fancy footwork and look for loopholes, decided a banjo might be the solution. Who wouldn't like to be able to play a banjo? A banjo looked like it would be fun and has a certain amount of cachet. How hard could it be? I'd seen hillbillies on *Heehaw* make it look easy. Even a comedian like Steve Martin learned to play a 5-string banjo. I didn't expect to be a virtuoso such as Earl Scruggs—just five easy pieces was all I wanted to be able to play.

After all, I had a little experience with a guitar. In the sixties, folk music and simple rock and roll songs were the rage and most involved guitars, and I decided to get one. Peanut Gilbert, a jack of all trades at the Western Auto store, sold me an off-brand guitar they had displayed there. The tone quality of this guitar was about what one would expect from a musical instrument purchased at an auto parts store. The sound it produced was like a fork scraping a pan.

Nevertheless, I joined several boys to take beginning guitar lessons at Wilma Stringer's house. Wilma, married to elementary principal Clifford "Mack" Stringer, taught freshman chorus and grade school music.

Wilma's guitar wasn't much better than mine, but she knew music and knew how to play a guitar. The lessons only lasted a few weeks, but we learned how to play a ditty called "Bill Grogan's Goat" and several three-chord songs.

My mind was doing the Texas two-step, now. Since I had plinked a guitar for a while and had some campfire songs and a few Beatle tunes in my repertoire, I thought I'd have a running start with a banjo.

Asking for help is always the last refuge for me, but I called a music store in the city and inquired about lessons. The owner said he provided instruction in bluegrass-style picking, and added that he could rent me a five-string banjo.

At my first lesson, I advised the instructor that I just wanted to learn five easy pieces, but in no time at all, I was convinced there *weren't* five easy pieces. Not on the banjo. Not even "Turkey in the Straw."

With a five-string banjo, the lower four strings extend from the bottom all the way to the top of the neck. The top string only goes about half-way up the neck and produces a high-pitched tone that is integral to the bluegrass sound.

With four strings on the upper neck and five on the bottom, my mind believes, and sabotages my hands into believing, that when my left hand is playing the top string on the neck that my right hand should be playing the top string on the bottom. Wrong. The top string on the bottom is the fifth (short) string. The result is piercing whine that sounds like a bullet ricocheting off a church bell, and I hit it often. I was beginning to think my instructor's frown lines would be permanent.

For the accomplished picker, the banjo is truly a musical instrument. For me, it is a neuro-motor skills appliance that challenges both sides of my brain. On the neck of the banjo, the right-brain controls the fingers of the left hand to make individual notes and chords. On the strumming part, the left brain manipulates curled fingers of the right hand in continuous rolling patterns. But getting the left hand and the right hand to work independently is like patting your head and rubbing your belly at the same time. It can be done but only with serious practice . . . and not by everyone.

Did a year of lessons improve my memory and mental faculties? As Mao Tse-tung supposedly said in remarking on the effect of the French Revolution—it's too soon to tell. But nonetheless, there are collateral benefits. I no longer fret about avoiding Sudoku and crossword puzzles, and I experience a lofty, insufferable smugness when a stranger sees my banjo case and wistfully says, "I always wanted to play the banjo."

Smugness is a precarious perch. As I was getting in my car after a lesson, my instructor hustled out of his studio waving some papers to get my attention. "Hey, professor, you forgot your music."

Maybe I should see if I can still play "Bill Grogan's Goat" on the guitar . . . or just give up and join the geezers at the courthouse.

Best Cat in the Solar System

IT RECENTLY CAME TO my attention that October 29th was National Cat Day. With the abounding number of odd "national" commemorative days, it isn't surprising that I missed it. But it caused me to reflect on some of the feline friends I've known.

Some folks don't like cats. Some claim to be only "dog people." And some don't like either. On the Shannon County farm where I spent much of my childhood, we had a variety of animals, including cats and dogs, and I like them both.

In one way or another, the animals on the farm earned their keep. Spot, a wiry, black and white terrier-mix, earned Grandpa's favor as a squirrel and rabbit dog. [Yes, we ate squirrels and rabbits, and I learned how to clean them at an early age. As cuisine, squirrels weren't bad, but rabbits, in my view, were another matter. I wouldn't give a nickel for a cooked rabbit on a plate, and I have eaten them in Paris and at fancy urban restaurants in the U.S. My wife cringes at the notion of eating either, and for now, I'm safe from hassenpfeffer.]

The cats on our farm weren't freeloaders, either. My grandma judged their worthiness on whether they were good "mousers," and let some live in the barn. I don't remember much about most of the barn cats except when I was handling the milking chores. I could aim in their direction and squirt them several feet away where they sat with their mouths open, lapping away. My grandmother frowned on this behavior, but where do you suppose I learned the trick?

You may recall that my grandpa wore a prosthetic, mechanical hook on one hand, which I don't think Ol' Bossy the cow would have appreciated. So, Grandma did most of the milking.

Two cats, Tom and Jerry, stood out from the pack. These two brothers looked nothing alike. Tom, a gray tabby, was skinny and skittish. My grandmother claimed, with some distain, it was because he ate lizards. Jerry, a cream-colored, husky boy, and a mouser by trade, was more favorably regarded by Grandma.

Jerry loved to be picked up, even by me as a 5-year-old. When cradled in my arms he draped from the middle like a loaf of bread. He even tolerated riding on my lap (as much as a cat could) as I peddled a tricycle in the front yard.

Jerry was my first cat buddy—there have been others— but I want to tell you about the current one—Bob.

On our security camera, two years ago in December, we saw a strange cat roaming through the woods in front of our house at 2 a.m. It was eerie. This gray tabby, with white boots and bib, was a double of our last cat, a shelter rescue named Nick Nolte. And this trespasser had just strolled past Nick's tombstone, a plump ceramic frog in a bikini.

My wife and I laughed that it was one of Nick's nine lives inspecting his old stomping grounds and didn't think much more about the incident. But then, the interloper showed up on the camera a second time. And a third. We began checking the camera every morning but didn't see him again.

A week later, a friend of mine who belongs to a cat rescue organization in St. Louis, and refers to herself as a "crazy cat lady," posted a photo on Facebook of a tomcat she had rescued and was fostering. This cat was also a ringer for Nick.

Two look-alikes in a week? Nah, I told myself, it couldn't be the same cat—St. Louis was 20 miles away. Brimming with curiosity, I emailed her to find out where she had found this cat. The answer astonished me.

A rescue colleague of hers, who lives only a mile from us, had been feeding feral cats. One in particular, whom she had named Bob, seemed less wild. Because of the frigid weather, they trapped him to get him into a shelter.

By the time I inquired, Bob had been accepted at a shelter in St. Charles County, which is 30 miles away. A couple days later, I had to be in St. Charles County on business, and a feeling that I can only describe as the sadness, drew me to the shelter.

Inside, Bob hunkered in a back corner on an elevated platform when I entered the room he shared with another cat. As my friend had posted on Facebook, he was "all big head and sad eyes—irresistible." Keeping a respectful distance, I stood without speaking, but our eyes locked in communication.

He didn't flinch as I approached and allowed me to pet his head. My heart told me this was a special cat. I said goodbye and silently vowed to return.

After the loss of Nick, we were hesitant to get another cat, but the next day my wife and I signed the adoption papers and took Bob home with us. We prepared a place in the guest bedroom as a safe space for him to become acclimated to his new home. At first, he hid under the bed and wouldn't come out when we were in the room. We knew it would take time to gain his trust.

Bob, the rescued tomcat, perched on his manservant's desk.

Several times a day I would enter Bob's room and lie on the bed, silently reading a book. On the third day, with no coaxing, Bob hopped onto the bed and stretched out near my feet. "Good, Bob," I said, but didn't attempt to pet him.

The following day he got on the bed and allowed me to pet him. The next day, within minutes of my lying down, he leaped onto the bed, crawled up on my chest, and stretched out facing me. He began purring and the muscles in his front paws alternately tensed and relaxed, as he peered into my eyes.

I paraphrased Humphrey Bogart's famous line from the movie *Casablanca*: "Bob, I think this is the beginning of a beautiful friendship." And it has been just that. Sometimes we slip and call him Nick, but we always tell him he is the best tomcat in the solar system.

Now, two years later, Bob has eased into an indoor life, living large and in charge, demanding to be brushed every day, and riding herd on two dogs. At night, if it's cold, he curls up on our bed, and during the day, he often perches on my desk as I write, occasionally assisting by tapping a few keystrokes. (Any typos are his fault.) And thanks to my talented sister-in-law, Sandra West Whitaker (WSHS '63), Bob even has his portrait painted on a rock.

It seems as if Bob has lived here for more than two years—maybe he has.

Lessons of Life and Green Tomato Mincemeat

IN MANY WAYS, THE 1950s lingered another five years beyond its closing date, keeping its hold on the first half of the sixties. Acid hadn't yet hit rock and roll, and folk music often topped the charts. Still, beatniks and coffeehouse poets preached that the times were changing.

But in 1962, times weren't changing much in Willow Springs. One thing, for sure, jobs for kids my age were scarce. I had mowed yards and hauled hay, but my first "salaried position" was working for Paul Hunter on the Holsum Bread truck.

I'd meet Paul at Shorty's B–B Café every Saturday morning at 6 a.m. and ride to Cabool to deliver bread to stores and restaurants. After returning and servicing the Willow stores, Paul would head back to Cabool leaving me to stack boxes at the warehouse and keep loaves straight on the store shelves. I earned $2.75—a day! After 6 months it was raised to $3.00.

It's weird how memories from the past, such as my working on a bread truck, can recur years in the future. Fifty-six years later at a writers' conference in Arkansas, a man introduced himself and said he wanted to give me a copy of his novel. I hadn't met him before, but he recognized me from participating on panels and emceeing one of the conference events.

His name tag indicated he was Sumner from Doolittle, MO. I mentioned that in high school, I worked for a bread truck driver from Doolittle, who had attended high school in the neighboring town, Newburg. "What was his name?" he asked. I told him the man was Paul Hunter. Sumner smiled and said, "He was in my class."

In the spring of 1962, the only significant change for me was turning 16 and acquiring a driver's license. Not long afterwards, I drove to Montier to visit my grade school buddy, Larry Stover. Larry had driven a tractor since the third grade and was a first-rate farmhand. The previous summer he had worked in the Kansas wheat harvest on a large farm owned by his sister Nadine and her husband Richard.

Larry thought he could get me hired. We sent a letter—the Stovers didn't have a phone—and got a reply that I had a job, which paid room and board and $1.25 an hour. I could barely imagine such a princely sum.

Nadine and Richard, with their two young children, picked us up at the bus depot in Wichita the night of our arrival in early June. As we rode 30 miles west to their farm near Cheney, Kansas, I realized that as hillbilly I had a limited understanding of flatness. And Kansas is definitely flat. Distances, particularly at night, are deceptive in much the same way the moon appears close but is really far away. Lights in the distance, which I thought were, maybe, 5 miles away, were 20 miles. Richard seemed to delight in pointing out the deceptive distances.

Harvesting wouldn't begin for a week, but we kept busy with general farm chores, including shoveling knee-deep manure out of a pig pen and battling biting flies, which had the attitude of Kamikazes, while I endured an abscessed tooth. Today, if I'm having a substellar day and want to put things in perspective, I sometimes think back to that day in the Kansas pig pen.

The farm had several tractors, including a nearly-new John Deere Model 2010, a 4-cylinder diesel with a cab that was the fanciest tractor I'd ever seen. To start it, a side-mounted "pony" engine, not much larger than a car battery, "jump started" the main engine simply by turning an ignition key.

Starting the tractor that I always drove, a 1933 John Deere, Model D, involved turning an 80-pound cast-iron flywheel by hand. Even as a strapping 16-year-old, it took all my strength. If the tractor stopped after it had been running, with pressure built up in the cylinders, the flywheel proved to be impossible to turn. Once, I tried when the two-cylinder beast stopped in the middle of a field. I grabbed the hot flywheel and jumped back with a handful of blisters.

Larry and I shared a bedroom in the farmhouse and ate with the family. Nadine furnished substantial meals coordinated around the work schedule. During harvest time, work was paramount. Breakfast consisted of cereal, milk, and eggs, after the morning chores. Afterwards, Larry and I plowed fields until the mid-day meal. Thank goodness for a transistor radio.

Lunch provided the sustaining meal of the day—the kind of meal fit for a threshing crew—such as fried chicken, green beans, potatoes, gravy . . . and pie. With the pie, I learned a lesson of life. Nadine set four large pieces on the table—two apple and two green tomato mincemeat. I had never heard of green tomato mincemeat pie and had little interest in trying it.

Larry, alert to the situation, grabbed a slice of the apple pie. Nadine, I suppose, because she baked it, selected green tomato mincemeat. That left two pieces—one apple and one green tomato mincemeat. Richard's questioning eyes met mine. On reflection, I have compared that moment to the "Battle over the Tea Cups," a short story my WSHS English class read, about a Chinese warlord and a traveler. While drinking tea, each tried to outmaneuver the other to keep from being poisoned.

Richard asked me which piece I wanted. Being polite (and thinking he would offer me the choice again), I told him to choose. And he did. He snatched the apple pie. He obviously didn't operate from the Code of Ozark Manners I had learned. Namely, after I offered him the choice, he was supposed say, "No, you go ahead." What did I learn? Know the rules before you play, and green tomato mincemeat pie must be an acquired taste.

Once the harvesting began, our days started at 5 a.m., and after lunch, we didn't eat supper until 9 or 10 at night, but Nadine brought us bologna sandwiches and Pepsis at 4 p.m. that we ate in the field. Larry, with his superior skill set, operated the combine, and Richard followed in a 2-ton dump truck collecting the harvested wheat. I plowed behind them turning over the wheat stubble for fall planting.

When the truck was full, either Richard or I drove 15 miles to the grain elevators in Garden Plain. As a 16-year-old with a newly acquired driver's license, whenever I drove, the importance of the responsibility weighed heavily on my mind, knowing

Richard and his family's livelihood for the year depended on getting the grain to market.

After the harvest, I spent $40 of my hard-earned cash on my first set of golf clubs. When I got home, I met one of Willow's best golfers, classmate Jimmy "Tee" Thomas, at the old course on Pine Grove Road for a lesson on golf—another acquired taste.

An Ozarker Abroad

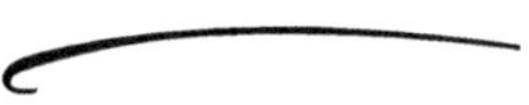

DURING MY JUNIOR YEAR at Mizzou, my friend Steve and I had two buddies who spent a summer in Europe. They returned with hair growing over their ears, which in 1967 in the Midwest was daring and radical, and fabulous tales of their adventures. Paris. Rome. Munich. And Rickey's Bar in Sitges, Spain.

Loaded with envy, we daydreamed of our own adventure in Europe the next summer. And the fact that WSHS classmate and fellow Mizzou student, Glenda Turner, had parlayed her musical talents into a job playing the piano at the Grosvenor Hotel in London, made the prospect seem possible.

However, I had another problem—the Selective Service. The only reason I hadn't been drafted was my 2-S student deferment, which every summer changed to 1-A—ready for service.

As a result, I had been discussing my future with the Marine Corps campus recruiter. I passed the aptitude tests and had an appointment with him to sign up for a program that would have me spending the next summer at the Office Candidates School in Quantico, Virginia.

On the morning of my appointment with the recruiter, I met Steve for coffee at the student union beforehand. With no uncertainty, he said, "You don't want to join the Marine Corps. Let's make a pact. Skip the Marine Corps and we'll go to Europe next summer." After some discussion, we shook hands, and I went to the lobby and told an upset recruiter I had changed my mind. [But I spent the summer of 1969, courtesy of the U.S. Army, at Ft. Benning, Georgia.]

We discovered a $300 roundtrip charter flight from St. Louis to London that departed in June and returned in late August. Our traveler friends told us about a $175 Eurail Pass that provided unlimited first-class train travel for two months. After scouring the popular travel book, *Europe on $5 a Day*, we estimated the cost to tour Europe would be about a $1,000 each. But how could we get that much money?

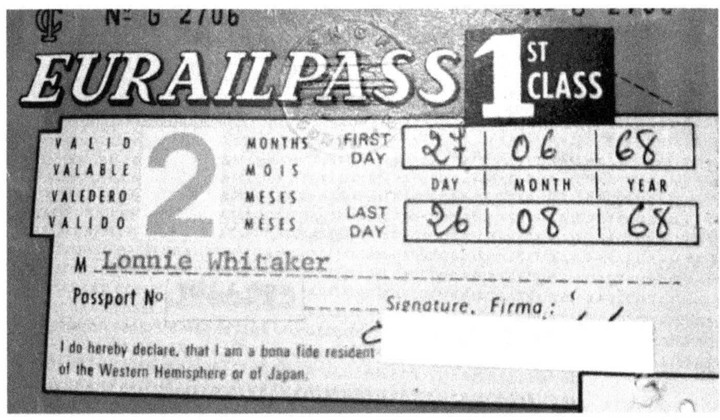

Lonnie Whitaker's 1968 Eurail Pass that provided two months' first-class train fare for continental Europe, excluding Greece.

We got parttime jobs. I stacked books at the University library, and Steve processed credit applications for a local loan company, but neither supplied enough dough to fund the trip. We started brainstorming. What if we could find a product to sell to students? Within the student population, we decided sororities and fraternities would be a prime market. Every spring the Greek organizations bought small keepsake gifts for their dates at spring parties. With a leap of imagination, we thought, perhaps, we could manufacture party favors for sororities?

We came up with idea of bath sarongs for men. A sarong is a garment consisting of a length of cloth wrapped around the body that ties at the waist. Basically, wrap-around towels with sewn-on Greek letters that girls could give to guys, who could wear them to the showers in the dorms or fraternity houses.

We brought Steve's girlfriend Susan, a home economics major and excellent seamstress, into the planning. For the fabric, we chose gold terrycloth (most sororities had gold as a color). She made prototypes, with sewn-on Greek letters, cut from felt, for two sororities: Kappa Alpha Theta and Delta Delta Delta. Both had spring events.

Steve's mother, Dorothy, dated a textile salesman who agreed to supply terrycloth at wholesale cost. Susan joined our venture as a partner for the major sewing responsibilities. All we needed to do was sell the sororities on the idea.

At that time in Columbia, a national jewelry company's representative named Troy Newman, had the market for party favors cornered. With his smooth South Carolina accent, he made the rounds to the Greek houses and essentially took orders. "Why, I sold this mug to your sisters at the University of South Carolina, and they just loved it. How many do you want?"

We had to beat Troy to the punch. I called the social chair-man at the Tri-delt house, and she told me I could make a presentation at a house meeting. Steve was out of town, so it would be a solo act. When I arrived, 50 meticulously-groomed women sat on the floor of a well-appointed living room waiting to hear my pitch. After I was introduced, the room became silent. Suddenly, I had stage fright.

I never know when my WSHS education is going to come into play, but on that evening, advice I had received from Raymond Newby, the speech and dramatics teacher at Willow, served me well. My senior year, Mr. Newby directed a three-act comedy play, *Adam's Evening*, which played for two nights to mostly sold-crowds in the WSHS auditorium. I played the title character, but classmate Buddy Stuart, demonstrating formidable acting chops, quickly became the crowd favorite playing the part of a whacky character.

Unlike Buddy, Mr. Newby sensed nervousness on my part to transform into the character. He bluntly said, "On stage, don't be Lonnie." In other words, hide behind the character.

That night at the Tri-delt house I became Troy Newman, the salesman from the South, albeit southern Missouri, and hawked the bath sarongs. I modeled them and did a little dance that I suspect looked more like an Ozark "double-shuffle." [I wish I had paid more attention to Willow banker, Joyce Burns, when he demonstrated his "old soft-shoe" for me.]

In the midst of all the laughter, the president called the room to order and by acclamation they voted to buy the sarongs for their Spring Steak Fry. We priced the sarongs at $15 apiece, and because we didn't have money for production costs, I collected a $5 deposit on each one.

My routine at the Tri-delts worked so well that Steve and I refined the act and went to the Theta house where it also worked. They agreed to buy the sarongs as party favors for their Theta Kite Flight event.

Several women who saw our product commented they would like a women's version. Susan designed a women's model, which tied below the arms, that we sold to the Sigma Alpha Epsilon fraternity, as date gifts for their "Plantation Ball."

With over $500 in deposits from our customers, we ordered the terrycloth and made arrangements to spend spring break at Dorothy's house in St. Louis. We planned to rent sewing machines after we got there.

Susan, Steve, and I arrived at Dorothy's and immediately arranged the basement into a workshop. That night we went to a fabric store and bought the felt. The next morning, we called everyplace we could think of that might rent sewing machines, with absolutely no luck. No place in St. Louis rented sewing machines.

How could we have made such a blunder in our planning? We had over $500 of our customers' money, bolts of terrycloth stacked in the basement, and no sewing machines. As my Irish grandmother might have said, "There's many a slip twixt the cup and the lip."

To be continued.

Ozarker Abroad, Part 2

PART 1 OF THIS article ended with my two partners and I in a predicament. We had collected a sizeable sum of money from our customers to manufacture bath sarongs as party favors, but discovered that we couldn't rent sewing machines, as we had planned.

With bolts of terrycloth stacked in the corner of the basement, cash deposits from our customers in hand, and unable to rent sewing machines to complete the job, we began to panic. But then we started brainstorming.

Since we couldn't rent sewing machines, what would it cost to buy a couple? After several telephone inquiries, it became obvious the cost would take most of the deposit money and our profits—goodbye trip to Europe. We considered just returning the deposit money, but again, no European trip, and with the specter of campus-wide embarrassment, we quickly tossed that notion aside. Maybe we could "borrow" two sewing machines.

I honestly don't recall who came up with the plan. It was risky, but out of a sense of desperation, we set it in motion.

Steve and Susan would pose as an engaged couple, with Susan wearing an old engagement ring borrowed from Steve's mom. The three of us drove to a Singer sewing machine store. As the "young couple" browsed in the store, a salesclerk offered his assistance. Susan explained they would be on a tight budget when they got married so she wanted save money by sewing.

After seeing several models, Susan indicated she liked one but just wasn't sure. The helpful salesman said, "Well, if you put down a small deposit, you can take it home and try it out for a week. If you don't like it, just bring it back and your deposit will be returned." We put the Singer in the trunk and headed for the Sears store at the other end of the shopping center.

Emboldened, with a routine down pat, we entered the Sears store. After selecting a model—it had to have zigzag stitch capability—Susan asked if they could try it out at home. The store manager said it could be tried at home for three days. Not as long as we needed, but nevertheless, Steve paid the deposit, and we put the Sears machine in the trunk and headed home. Time to get to work.

We spent the first couple days and nights cutting Greek letters out of felt and making templates from posterboard to align the letters on the sarongs. In our manufacturing shop in a corner of the basement, we set up an assembly line.

For some reason, the basement had a table with a butcher paper roller mounted on one end that worked perfectly with terrycloth bolts. Steve would roll out a section of cloth, cut it with the electric scissors, place the carboard template over the fabric, and pin the felt letters to the cloth. He stacked it next to Susan who sewed on the letters.

I had never operated a sewing machine before, and the only one I ever remember seeing in use was my grandmother's the pedal-operated antique. But after some instruction from Susan, I got the hang of it. When Susan finished with the letters, she handed the sarong to me to sew on Velcro strips, which served as fasteners.

Our design was "one size fits all." We used the same amount of fabric on each sarong, with the size determined by the positioning of the Velcro strips. Each order specified the size—small, medium, or large. Buttonholes would have been too complicated and time consuming.

While many college friends spent spring vacation on the beaches in Florida, we spent long days and nights in the basement sewing and listening to top-40 music and the syndicated adventures of Chickenman, a takeoff from the Batman TV series.

For those who are unfamiliar with Chickenman, each crime-solving episode of the "Fantastic Fowl" started with the shrill call of a chicken followed by voices yelling, "He's everywhere! He's everywhere!" What can I say? We were looking for any diversion from sewing. But the song that seemed to play most often was "Leaving on a Jet Plane" by Peter, Paul and Mary, and that became our theme song.

Sometime in the middle of the week, as we toiled away in our basement workshop, from upstairs, we heard the doorbell ring. The front door was equipped with an intercom, and a voice came through the inside speaker. "This is Mr. 'Smith' from the Sears store. I've come to get the sewing machine. It was due back yesterday."

We hid silently in the basement. We needed the Sears machine for a few more days. Mr. Smith rang the doorbell several times more before finally leaving. Then we got concerned that Mr. Smith would return with the police, but calmed ourselves that we weren't really criminals, by applying the playground rule: no harm, no foul. But as (future) lawyers, Steve and I had never heard of larceny by trick or *trespass de bonis asportatis.* (If you take someone's property, an action will lie even if you return it, because you have deprived the person on its use).

By the end of Spring Break, we completed the manufacturing, returned the sewing machines (with no problems), and delivered the goods to our customers on time. I don't recall that we received even one complaint. But most importantly, we collected a bunch of money and were well on our way to financing the trip

Just as our plane took off for London, almost poetically, "Leaving on a Jet Plane" played over the intercom. And after a raucous flight, full of imbibing college students, we landed at Heathrow Airport on June 14, 1968, ready to begin a most memorable summer.

And thank goodness for the Statute of Limitations.

Basketball Memories—Part 1

THE OLD WSHS GYMNASIUM has always reminded me of a swimming pool, a natatorium of the 1930s, set below street level and surrounded above by concrete bleachers with backless, slatted seats. Reprising the lines of the school song, it was "a place of many blessed memories."

With the smell of FFA popcorn in the air, and the cacophony of fans and cheerleaders yelling for the Bear hoopsters, men named Munford, Ledgerwood, Copeland, Shanahan, Scott, and Martin coached teams there in the last century.

The old gym has some unique synchronicities, or crossing of paths, worthy of noting. One, for example, is coach L. Joe Scott and one of his players, Billy Shanks (WSHS, '66). Both received all-Ozark and all-state honors, but also hold records for individually scoring over 50 points in one high school basketball game.

It's fair to say that no basketball coach ever arrived in Willow Springs with a pedigree matching that of Joe Scott. As a three-year letterman at the University of Missouri (freshman were not allowed to play on the varsity), captain of the team, and all-Big 8 selection, he set the Mizzou single game scoring record, tallying 46 points against Nebraska his senior year in 1961. Moreover, he scored 1,128 career points, which ranks him number 35 for career scoring at Mizzou.

His single game record still stands, and this was before the 3-point shot. Based on Joe's shooting range, one teammate suggested if there had been a 3-point line back then he would have scored closer to 60 points. A highlight film of that remarkable shooting display can be seen online.

Joe was no stranger to the Ozarks. He went to high school in Gainesville, Missouri, where he led his basketball team to the "final four" in the Class M state tournament in 1957. According to the Missouri Sports Hall of Fame website, he averaged over 30 points a game his senior year, with a career total over 1,100 points, and earned first-team all-state and first-team all-Ozark honors.

Nor, was Joe a stranger to Willow Springs basketball. On February 19, 1957, the Bears played Gainesville. Recently, I spoke with Willow's favorite son, Wendell Bailey, who said, "I have some personal knowledge about that game. I rode with coach Johnny Ledgerwood on the yellow school bus to Gainesville. We played in the old gym, that I called a 'cracker box' of a small gym. That is where you put one foot behind you on the wall to throw in the ball." [I played in that gym in Gainesville, and Wendell does not exaggerate.]

Of that game, Wendell says, "I was a junior and L. Joe Scott was a 6'4" senior, called the 'Gainesville Gunner.' Joe would take the ball out of bounds, throw it in and take a pass back and shoot one of his noted jump shots. I told the Springfield newspaper that I did a pretty good job guarding Joe, and he ran in 58 points that night." Missouri State High School Athletic Association statistics, indicate that Joe Scott had 41 field goal attempts that night, which ties for ninth place in Missouri high school records.

The 1962-63 WSHS basketball team wearing the striped knee socks Coach Scott acquired. *Photo is from the 1963 Willamizzou.*

As an aside, Wendell noted that Coach Ledgerwood had experience with high scorers. Before coming to Willow, he coached J. D. Boyer at Winona who later scored 92 points against Freemont in October 1958, which is the record for the most points scored ever in a Missouri high school game. Boyer also holds the record for the most field goals attempted (53) in a game. Incidentally, I posted a Facebook query on a Shannon County group, and J.D. Boyer is still remembered and held in high regard.

Another interesting coincidence: Richard Beavers, who played on Scott's Willow team, became a successful area high school basketball coach and was named 2A Coach of the Year in 1988, after taking Liberty (Mountain View–Birch Tree) to second place in the state tournament. Richard started his coaching career at Winona.

Joe Scott arrived in Willow Springs in 1962, along with his fiancé, Judith Wangelin, the summer before he became the basketball coach in the fall. Joe coached the summer league baseball teams, which is where I first met him. One word described him—cool. Six-foot-four, movie star-handsome, and loaded with confidence, a trait he imparted to his teams.

That summer, fiancé Judy lived with Allen and Hazel Frazee and taught swimming and lifesaving lessons at Smokey Stover's covered swimming pool. I took intermediate swimming and junior lifesaving from her. In one of the classes, she made us swim one mile to pass—it must have been 60 lengths of that pool.

The 1962–63 Willow basketball team only had two seniors, David James and George Stanton. Juniors, Mike Warning (the tallest player at 6'5") and Richard Beavers (a ferocious rebounding forward) and sophomore shooting guard Truman Grogan rounded out the starting five. Although the team only finished fifth in the SCA Conference, David James led the SCA in scoring, with 269 points.

A remarkably talented athlete, David James could shoot with either hand and had great jumping ability. Driving in for a layup, he could leap toward the basket from near the free throw line, and while in mid-air, flip the ball from one outstretched hand to the other before shooting. And although not the tallest player on the team at 6'3", he "jumped center" at tipoffs.

Surprisingly, four players on that team played basketball in college: David James at William Jewell; Richard Beavers at

Southwest Baptist College, and later, at Arkansas College (now, Lyon College); Bill Shanks at the University of Missouri at Rolla, and as I recall but can't confirm, Mike Warning played at Southeast Missouri State.

A couple weeks ago, I chatted with Joe Scott, now a Poplar Bluff attorney, and he remembered his time in Willow fondly. He inquired about several of his former players, and then asked me if I remembered the knee socks that we wore as part of our uniforms. I told him I did and recalled how proud we were of them—at the time they were uber-cool. Then, he told the backstory to the stockings.

Halfway through the season, the Bears had lost five games in a row, when Joe and Judy went to Poplar Bluff to visit relatives. While there, Joe visited a local sporting goods store and had a conversation with the owner who told him the team needed a jumpstart. He said the maroon and white-striped tube socks on display in his store would be just the ticket. Poplar Bluff High School has the same school colors as Willow Springs.

Joe liked the socks, but said he couldn't afford them, and did not have authority to purchase them on behalf of the school. The owner said, "I'll give you an invoice, and if the school doesn't want to pay it, tell them I'll donate them." Joe didn't say, but I assume superintendent T.G. Munford coughed up the money.

After Joe told the story, he laughed and said, "I was over-coaching at the time. I had a play for every situation. But after I got the socks, I quit coaching [so hard] and we won three games in a row."

To be continued.

Basketball Memories—Part 2

IN THE PREVIOUS ARTICLE, I mentioned connections, in various "degrees of separation," between the old Willow Springs gymnasium and high-scoring basketball players in the Ozarks. One example was Richard Beavers (WSHS 1964) coaching at Winona, the same school where Willow Coach Johnny Ledgerwood had coached, and J.D. Boyer set the Missouri single game scoring record.

After reading my article, Richard contacted me and shared information about another high-flying performance. "I also coached a young man at Winona who scored big. Jackson Lloyd is 18th in the MSHSAA [Missouri State High School Activities Association] individual scoring in a game with 61 points in 1969."

Willow had its own record-setting scorer—a teammate of Richard and mine—Billy Shanks (WSHS 1966). I saw Billy Shanks for the first time when my junior high basketball team played Pomona, I'm not sure which team won, but I do recall the game provided a greater challenge than anticipated.

Perhaps we wondered how little Pomona could compete against the mighty Cubs. Well, Pomona seventh-grader Billy Shanks showed us how. After the game, Coach Buddy Bennett said "That Shanks boy really has a soft touch."

Two years later, playing on the same team with Billy, reinforced Buddy Bennett's description of his shooting. When David James or Truman Grogan took shots, the basketballs ripped through the net, as if they had been thrown. When the ball left Billy's hands, it ascended with a high arc floating toward the goal before descending with a whisper through the net.

Bill had significant accomplishments off the basketball court. Elected class president as a junior, he was also chosen student council vice president the same year. Among many academic accomplishments, he scored in the upper ten percentile in the Missouri State-wide Aptitude Test. It isn't surprising he parlayed his studies at the University of Missouri at Rolla into a successful career as an engineer.

Bill had natural athletic ability and could have excelled at other sports, but he focused on basketball. His junior year, he was selected first-team all-SCA. As a senior, he, again, earned first-team all-conference status, as well as being named SCA's Most Valuable Player. Moreover, he achieved honorable mention all-Ozark and all-state honorable mention.

He earned a varsity letter as freshman under Coach Joe Scott, but he secured a starting spot for the next three years with a new coach, Bob Martin.

After coaching for two seasons at Fair Grove, Missouri, Coach Martin arrived in Willow the summer of 1963, with his wife and two infant sons. Like many new coaches, he ran the youth baseball programs.

A product of the Ozarks, Bob Martin lettered four years in high school at Lockwood, Missouri. After high school, he played basketball and received an associate of arts degree at Southwest Baptist College in Bolivar. He finished his undergraduate education at Southwest Missouri State (SMS), where he played basketball.

Basketball wasn't the only highlight of his college days. He sang his way onto the cast of the SMS production of the Broadway play, "Finnian's Rainbow." The production was selected for a seven-week USO tour to entertain troops in Europe in 1961. Martin says, "I was offered the chance to go on the USO tour, but I got married in June following graduation, and the tour overlapped the wedding date."

Coach Martin could definitely sing. He sat next to me in the tenor section of the First Baptist choir. He once joked that if God didn't let sing him bass in Heaven that he wouldn't sing in the choir. But in a recent conversation, he laughed and told me his position has softened.

Coach Martin had insight that transcended diagraming plays, and offered encouragement to players to expand their vision. As the assistant track coach my junior year, he challenged me to join the track team. I wasn't a fast runner and didn't see much opportunity, but he guaranteed me a medal at the conference track meet if I would throw the discus.

I took his challenge as a dare and agreed to participate, in part, to prove him wrong. He won the challenge. I came in second place in the SCA meet and got a silver medal. He saw potential in me that I didn't see in myself. That's what a good coach does.

With three returning starters, plus Shanks, the Bears won 13 games against 12 losses in Martin's first season, with two significant accomplishments: a second-place trophy at the Cabool Tournament, and beating archrival West Plains for the first time in 28 years.

Oddly, the next year in the '64-'65 season, the Bears reversed the wins and losses from the previous season, with a 12 and 13 record. Highlights included Shanks racking up two 30-point games and being the only junior named to the first-team, all-SCA. Johnny Jones and Truman Grogan (both, WSHS 1965) received honorable mention all-SCA honors.

But the pinnacle of the Coach Martin/Billy Shanks era, may have happened at home in the 1965-1966 season when Shanks set the school and conference single game record with 51 points (70% of the Willow 73 points) against Houston.

John McGlynn and Johnny Jones, two of my 1965 classmates, attended that game on January 25, 1966, and had seats behind the Houston bench. McGlynn says, "Houston had one guy pick up Bill at half court, and a second player when Bill was at the top of the key. And if Bill started to drive to the basket, a third guy joined in, and Bill ate their lunch."

In a recent phone conversation, Coach Martin recalled that game when there were only a few seconds left on the clock. "We were down by three points, with Shanks at the free throw line shooting two. I told him to make the first shot and miss the second so we'd have a chance at the rebound. I told him the way to miss the second was to shoot the ball with a flatter trajectory. He made the first. The second bounced off the back of the rim and over the head of our guy in the middle." The game ended with a Houston win, 75-73.

I contacted Bill about his recollection of that night. "I don't remember a lot about the night I scored 51 points other than I had a somewhat normal first half and then got hot in the second half (one of those times when everything went in). The Houston players seemed to get frustrated in the second half and started fouling a lot, which made for some easy scores."

Fouling Bill wasn't a good idea, since he was a 90-percent free throw artist. Apparently, the Tigers didn't learn their lesson, because in the return match at Houston in February, Bill sank 25 foul shots, which ties for third place in the MSHSAA records for free throws made in a single game.

For every time there is a season. French Lick had Larry Bird; Gainesville had Joe Scott; Winona had J.D. Boyer; and Willow was blessed to have Billy Shanks.

Powderpuff and the Evolution
of Women's Sports

IN SEVERAL PREVIOUS ARTICLES, I focused on men's sports, mostly football and basketball, but a few recent events, including a federal executive order, shifted my thoughts to the progress that has been made in women's sports.

The Willow Springs school song has the words ". . . playing basketball. . .", but in the 1950s and 1960s, it only applied to boys. Opportunities for girls to participate on sports teams did not exist. Cheerleading, marching band, and physical education classes provided the only athletic outlets.

Catherine (Beavers) Weekly (WSHS, 1960), who moved to Willow as a freshman, says she played on basketball teams in junior high in Arkansas and missed not being able to play in high school.

And Willow Springs had girls who could have excelled. When I spoke to former basketball coach Joe Scott a few weeks ago, he independently recalled—from 50 years before—that his player Billy Shanks had an older sister in PE classes that had remarkable athletic ability. I told him that was Trudy Shanks (WSHS, 1963), and that Coach Buddy Bennett once said she could have made the boys' track team.

Classmate Sandy (Merrill) Grogan, athletic as well, (in the eighth grade, she could prance on her tiptoes like a ballerina) said, "Trudy Shanks could probably outrun any boy in school but as there was no track team for us, we'll never know. In PE we would run, and I was thrilled if I could tie her. Not having girls' sports was a big disappointment to me, and I still get a little bitter taste about it."

The situation changed in the 1970s, and from the sports pages of the Howell County News, I have noticed, with the success of the Willow Springs Lady Bears in basketball, softball, and volleyball, that the progress continues. As of this writing, the Lady Bears basketball team is charging toward winning the SCA conference and is ranked 21st in the state for Class 4 schools. Go Lady Bears!

My wife played competitive team basketball from junior high through college, at St. Louis University. She likes to point out that they used the same size ball as the men. In 1984, the size of the basketball became an inch smaller for women, which makes it interesting to consider, that basketball for women prior to the 1970s was a game today's Lady Bears would hardly recognize.

The first time I realized that the rules for women's basket-ball, even in the 1960s, were different from the men's game was during my freshman year in 1961. Physical education teacher Wilma Stringer organized a women's basketball team to play an exhibition game in the old gym. I am not certain, but I think it was the same night the Class of 1962 arranged a game between the local town team and the Harlem Stars, a professional Harlem Globetrotter-type team.

Two things come to mind about that night. Coach Buddy Bennett trying to guard a Harlem Stars player, who bounced the ball to himself through Buddy's legs and went in for an uncontested layup. I think Buddy laughed harder than the spectators. And the weird rules for women's basketball.

Under the old rules, women teams had six players instead of five, three guards, who only defended and didn't shoot, and 3 shooting forwards. The floor was divided into two halves, offensive and defensive. The forwards (shooters) of one team would be located on the side of the court where the other team's guards were stationed. All shots from the floor counted two points. Until the early 1950s, unlimited dribbling was not allowed. After a player got the ball, it could only be bounced twice.

As the saying goes, what's old is new again. Old-fashioned women's basketball has returned to popularity as "Granny Basketball." [I'm not being insensitive; it is a trademarked term.] It started in Iowa in 2005, but has made its way to Missouri. It's billed as competitive exercise for women over the age of 50 and a method of preserving six-on-six basketball.

The typical granny uniforms are loose-fitting blouses, with sailor neckerchiefs, and bloomers with stockings. I suggested to my wife that she might be interested in joining a team. She questioned what planet I came from.

In the sixties, girls might not have been able to compete in team basketball, volleyball, or track at WSHS, but in 1963, the junior and senior girls played each other in football—powder-puff football. Proceeds from the sale of tickets helped fund the senior class trip.

Powderpuff football is a variation of touch football played by women. Rather than tackling a runner with the ball, the opponent grabs a strip of cloth ("flag") hanging from a runner's pants pocket or belt. Or as Sandy Grogan, one of the stars of the game, recently told me, "Even though I was a cheerleader, I didn't know much about football mechanics. So, you guys would tell us what to do, but I think all of us knew to just try to get that ball and tackle (flag) anyone who had it."

I have searched and failed to find a photograph of the game, but I do have eyewitness accounts, most indicating the scrimmage failed to match the image of the name. That is, it wasn't very "powder puffery." In fact, it involved trickery, scuffles, and injuries.

Barbara (Sherrill) Pigg (WSHS, 1964) recalls, "Football players were coaching both teams and I remember we injured two players during practice, and Coach [Case] wouldn't let the team help us anymore. I think Dan Zimmerman ended up on crutches for a while."

Peggy (Henry) Bradford (WSHS, 1965) says, "As for the powderpuff football game, I couldn't forget that one. Someone that shall remain nameless hit me on the nose and the resulting nosebleed ended the game for me. Not much powderpuff about that game, as I remember someone later being carried off on a stretcher. That was quite a night."

As to the trickery, Barbara says, "Judy R. also played and tied a rock to her flag, and with tight jeans or maybe jean shorts, it didn't pull out easily. I think Sandy pulled it out and the small rock hit her in the face." According to Barbara, the two girls ended up in a shirt-grabbing tussle. Sandy confirmed she was in the scrap.

With all the rule changes, transitions, and progress—from PE only to 5-player women's basketball—one thing I know for sure: after my wife's reaction, I will not suggest that any of the powderpuff players take up Granny Basketball.

An Ozark Girl's Golf Odyssey

WITH THE MASTERS GOLF tournament just around the corner, and my last article about the transition of women's high school sports still in the back of my mind, I thought of golf professional Jo D. Duncan Armstrong. You haven't heard of her? Just keep reading.

In the 1960s, WSHS had a boy's golf team, with classmate Jimmy "Tee" Thomas usually leading the pack, but no girls played on the team. Perhaps that lends credence to the notion that golf is an acronym meaning: Gentlemen Only Ladies Forbidden.

For the record, that adage wasn't true on the old 9–hole course with sand greens on Pine Grove Road in Willow Springs. In the 1960s, Celia Burns, Ruby Tetrick, Freda Lovan, and other women were ardent and accomplished regulars. Celia once told me the ball would go farther if I didn't swing so hard. I often recall her advice, after swinging like mighty "Casey at the Bat."

Nor, was that the case in 1984 at McDonald County High School in Anderson, MO, where Jo D. ("Jody") Duncan was a senior. That year, MCHS added golf to its varsity curriculum.

With moxie and pluck, Jody joined the team as the only girl. Moreover, she was the only female in the Big Six Conference (now, Southwest Conference) to complete on varsity boys' teams. And compete she did. She had the second-best scoring average on her team.

One local publication called her a trailblazer and reported that her coach, David Riffle, was glad she was on the team, regardless of her gender, because she was one of the better players in the area.

In the 1980s, before joining the high school team, Jody played golf at the Elk River Country Club near Noel, MO. She says of the old nine-hole course, "Along holes 2 and 3 there was a cow pasture, so there was a lot of entertainment."

Nevertheless, her golfing skills earned her a scholarship at Southwest Missouri State University. Remarkably, playing in college marked the first time she competed against other females.

After graduation from college, she taught at several schools in southwest Missouri before becoming the head basketball and golf coach for boys and girls at Metro Christian Academy in Tulsa, OK, in 1990.

In the early 1990s, she returned to golf fulltime and sampled life as a playing professional. But without sponsors, driving from tournament to tournament is a tedious and expensive grind. Ultimately, she found her niche in golf as the Director of Instruction at Norwood Hills Country Club in St. Louis. It some ways, Norwood provided the best of both worlds. It enabled her to teach—her first love—and allowed time to play in tournaments.

In November 2005, Jody hit a long shot when she secured a spot on The Golf Channel's Big Break V, a reality television show that would be filmed on Oahu's north shore in Hawaii. Select women golfers would be pitted against each other in a five-day skills competition for professional tour exemptions and prizes, including a new Chrysler Crossfire and a year's travel expenses for tour competition.

Reality TV shows are common, but imagine the odds of actually making it on one. Jody emerged from over 4000 applicants as one of eleven women receiving an expense paid trip to Hawaii and the opportunity to compete.

Of the fierce competition, Jody says, "The finalists included two first-team all-Americans; a U.S. Women's Amateur champion; and a two-time Australian Tour champion. I was the dark-horse candidate . . . and the oldest."

The application process took four months, from May to September, culminating with an interview in Maryland that included an "on-command" skills demonstration. Jody says, "It wasn't just swinging a three-wood a few times, we were told to hit a high fade or draw so many feet to the right or left of a target. It was a lot of pressure. If you were having an off-day it was too bad."

With this level of intensity and competition, how was she able to gain an edge? This wasn't her first exposure to national television competition. Jody competed in the World Long Drive Championship for several years, and won second place in 2001. Her longest competitive drive was 315 yards. I suspect with today's advanced equipment technology, it would have been longer.

She also thinks her application video helped distinguish her. Playing up her Ozark heritage, she appeared wearing a gingham blouse in lieu of a golf shirt. She said, "I stopped short of using a corncob pipe as a stage prop."

The contestants received a huge surprise before they had unpacked their bags. They were shocked to learn the application process wasn't over yet. There were eleven women, but accommodations for only ten.

A series of contests ending in a sudden-death play-off would send one woman home. "I couldn't believe it," Jody says, "We had to play our way into a bed."

The first play-in challenge involved chipping balls to break glass panels bearing the names of contestants. When a woman's panel was broken, she was eliminated from that challenge. The last unbroken panel designated a "bed-winner."

Clearly the star of the glass-breaking challenge, Jody broke five panels—twice as many as anyone else. One of her competitors said, "Jody seemed unbeatable." But, with only two players left, a woman who hadn't broken one panel managed to hit the corner of Jody's panel, winning immunity for herself and leaving Jody to compete for a spot on the show.

Jody is good, but no golfer is immune from the fickle ways of the Golf Gods. She went from being the first-round leader to missing the final cut. In the sudden-death finale, she was eliminated when her putt stopped a few feet short of the cup.

Another surprise. Jody wasn't really sent home. She was hidden from the others in a hotel and later would be given a mulligan—a chance to play her way back into the contest.

While the other women were anguishing over flubbed shots, Jody was being escorted around Oahu for several days as a tourist. She says, "Being eliminated first, turned out to be a blessing in disguise. I saw much more than the other girls. I went to Pearl Harbor and toured the U.S.S. Missouri and the Arizona Memorial—I really wanted to see that."

The mulligan didn't pan out, but the highlight for Jody wasn't about herself. She says, "My proudest moment was winning $5000.00 for The Brain Injury Foundation of St. Louis in a chip, putt, and drive contest involving local junior golfers."

How will they keep her "down on the farm" after seeing Hawaii? Jody says, "I'm lucky. I got to come back to the greatest job in the world. I love what I do."

There's a twilight on a golf course defined not so much by the sun, but by the solitude. The members have gone and the caddy shack kids can get in a few holes. The driving range is empty, but after a day of instructing others, that's where you'll often find Jody, working on her game—and she's got game.

Mr. Fred Thomas—Part 1

IF YOU ATTENDED SCHOOL in Willow Springs in the 1950s and 1960s, chances are you experienced Fred Thomas in some fashion. In my mind's eye, I still see him as the WSHS principal, a sixty-something man with mostly gray hair, never perfectly combed unless he was sporting a flattop, wearing a rumpled brown suit, as a requirement of the job and not by preference.

I remember the wry smile and twinkle in his eye that let you know he was aware of the latest shenanigan afoot—a proverbial Dutch uncle who could spot a fib before it passed the lips of a squirming student.

Mr. Thomas joined the school faculty as an

WSHS Principal Fred Thomas.
Photo is from the 1963 Willamizzou.

eighth-grade teacher and elementary principal in 1949, and assumed duties as high school principal in 1957, along with teaching World Geography. He cast a long shadow over the Willow School system, but civic and business activities occupied his "spare" time. He served as Rotary Club president in 1963 and owned a grocery store in Hutton Valley.

Classmate Peggy Henry Bradford (WSHS, 1965) remembers the Hutton Valley store well. Not surprisingly, since Mr. Thomas married her father's sister, Violet Henry Thomas. She says, "The country store in Hutton Valley, one with a big stove and long bench beside it, was a gathering place for many in the area. I spent a lot of time with my Aunt Violet after my mother went to work at the baby shoe factory in Willow Springs. It was my drop-off and pick-up place."

When he taught the 8th grade, Mr. Thomas is remembered fondly by former students for reading stories to them. John Tandy (WSHS, 1960) says, "Mr. Thomas was wonderful closing out the classroom day reading the class a classic book. Stopping for moments to ask questions to the class like, 'Now why do you think Tom Sawyer did that?'" With four children of his own, he, no doubt, had considerable experience reading to kids. By the time I was in high school, he had 7 grandchildren.

But woe to the student who tried to take advantage of his good nature. He could be a formidable nemesis, and when it came to discipline, he was not a "respecter of persons." Popular student or ruffian, he meted out punishment equally.

Consider the case of "The Sabotaged Bells" and outstanding student John Tandy. Athlete, musician, and student council president, he is mentioned 12 separate times in the 1960 *Willa-mizzou*—one photo covers the entire page. Moreover, his father, Captain John Tandy, commanded Missouri Highway Patrol Troop G and was one of the most respected men in Willow Springs. But first, a backstory from his classmate, Catherine Beavers.

Catherine says when they were seniors the school bell system that signaled the beginning and ending of classes was manipulated by Tandy and Robert Curtis (WSHS, 1960). Today, the motivation is somewhat uncertain, but the intent may have been to shorten one class they didn't like and lengthen Government class that they did like. "Well, somehow, it wasn't done right, and everyone got out of school 20 minutes early."

Catherine didn't recall any punishment resulting from the prank, but after the graduation ceremony, students still had to go to the principal's office to pick up their actual diplomas. However, when she went to the office to get her diploma, she says, "Mr. Thomas asked me if I knew who changed the bell. I replied, 'Yes, sir, I do.' He asked if I was going to tell him. I replied, 'No, sir.' He said, 'That's okay, Cathy,' and started laughing.

Catherine continued her reflection on the incident. "When John and Robert came in to get their diplomas, Mr. Thomas made them stand and stare at the clock for 20 minutes before he gave them their diplomas."

I checked with culprit John Tandy, and his memory differs slightly but confirms the incident. John says, "The story about the school bell is true unfortunately. The school 'let out bell' rang about 20-30 minutes early that day. Why would any student question the 'get out of class free' bell? So, everyone began leaving the building."

John expanded on how the caper developed. "Now that my friend Robert Curtis can't challenge my recollection of that day, I can tell you the 'truth.' Robert approached me in the hallway and said that the principal's office was vacant, and that we should sneak in and 'look around.' We did and he quickly found the big alarm clock bell. Wouldn't it be funny if school was let out about 10 minutes early! And why not in the minds of two Rock Hudson look-alikes!"

Now, the question remains, was John mostly an innocent bystander or a co-conspirator? In his defense, John says, "Truthfully, I didn't think Robert would reset the clock, but he did and shot out of the office to get back in class. Try to think how you would feel at that moment in time? I am standing alongside the principal's desk by myself, looking at the big reset clock on the wall with its glass door open wide. What would anyone do? I ran away from the crime scene and tried to contemplate what would happen next. The rest is history."

But wait, there's more. As an afterthought, John added, "I am a little sketchy on the rest of the story, but I do remember being called to the principal's office several weeks later, where an assistant principal showed Robert and me the old rugged paddle hanging from a wall, and telling me to bend over. I learned quickly why paddles have holes drilled in them."

In today's litigious world, an incident like the Sabotaged Bells might well involve lawyers, lawsuits, and hard feelings. Back then, we had our own version of Solomon evenhandedly dispensing justice. It's odd, but I don't recall even the ruffians or the boys Mr. Thomas caught skipping school in Doc's poolhall harboring grudges against him. But that's the way we were.

A sad afternote. Condolences to the friends and family of Robert Curtis who recently passed away. He sold me numerous items at the Curtis clothing store, and I occasionally worked with him there during the holiday season. Although he was five years older, he always treated me in a friendly and considerate manner. Rest in peace, Robert.

Mr. Fred Thomas—Part 2

MUCH OF THE PREVIOUS article about Fred Thomas, the long-time teacher and principal in Willow Springs, focused on his good humor and evenhanded disposition. In that light, classmate John McGlynn recalls an incident when Mr. Thomas monitored study hall.

In the 1960s, the study hall occupied the south half of the library room on the second floor of the old high school building. The teacher proctoring the study hall sat at a desk near the entrance to the library at the back of the room. On occasion, Mr. Thomas rode herd on the students there, who often pretended to be studying, as they whispered and passed notes.

On this particular day, John says Mr. Thomas left the room and returned to his office across the hall to attend to other business. In his absence, John and a couple cohorts began singing a ditty they had heard on Chicago radio station WLS: "Better Get Ready for Freddy, Because Freddy is Ready for You."

A couple refrains by the songsters and laughter from the other students prompted Mr. Thomas to hustle back. John says,

"Mr. Thomas tried to act like he was mad, but we could tell he really wasn't. He finally laughed, too."

A sidenote about WLS. With FM radio nonexistent in Howell County in the 1960s, radio reception during the day in Willow Springs mainly came from local station KUKU. But pursuant to Federal Communication Commission rules the broadcast signed off at sundown, and teenagers cruising Main Street from the "Little Y" to the Daisy Queen listened to rock and roll and the antics of disc jockey Dick Biondi on 50,000-watt Clear Channel WLS.

Classmate Peggy (Henry) Bradford remembers an incident involving Mr. Thomas when her former grade school in Hutton Valley was about to be closed. "My mother told me if I wanted to visit my old school again, time was growing short. So, my friend Sandy (Merrill) Grogan and I decided to skip school and go to Hutton Valley for the day. We visited the school and stopped by Violet's [Mr. Thomas's wife] store on our way home and she gave us some ice cream. We were sitting on the front porch of the store eating our ice cream when Fred came home from school in Willow. He got out of his car and told us in his very serious voice we were going to be removed from the cheerleading squad for skipping school. I knew he was kidding, but Sandy didn't, and I found out from Sandy many years later how she worried about being kicked off the squad."

Barbara (Sherrill) Pigg recently shared a surprising occurrence when Mr. Thomas chaperoned the Class of '64 senior trip to Biloxi, Mississippi. While there, students boarded a ferry to Ship Island to play in the ocean. Barbara says, "We got off the boat and everyone started taking off T-shirts and beach coverups."

Mr. Thomas approached and was talking to her and Dick Pigg, but turned his back to them and proceeded to take off his shoes, socks, white dress shirt, undershirt, and his pants, while she and Dick stood there in shock. He wore swimming trunks underneath his pants, but I can imagine their surprise. They may have felt the way I did when I saw Mrs. Munford in brush rollers in my mother's beauty shop.

Barbara said, "He enjoyed the water as much as our classmates. It was so strange to see him undress on the beach. He was so much fun away from the school."

In general, Mr. Thomas had a measured, and sometimes creative, approach to discipline. During my sophomore year, wearing football jerseys as a fashion statement became popular, but the availability of jerseys was scarce.

As a result of the popular demand, football jerseys began disappearing from the storage closet in the gym, and players could be spotted wearing them after school and on weekends. Coach Robert Lee reported the problem to Mr. Thomas. It wasn't just a few missing jerseys—the cupboard was practically empty.

Like a territorial governor in the Old West, Mr. Thomas posted a notice of clemency to the "outlaws." The jerseys could be returned to a cardboard box in his office without punishment, and no questions would be asked. But anyone caught with a jersey after the grace period would be expelled from school. The clemency box that sat next to secretary Naida Protiva's desk filled up in short order. I turned in mine, and so did everyone I knew who had a purloined jersey.

But some circumstances could try Mr. Thomas's patience, and his countenance would turn flinty. One such instance occurred when a few student pranksters, who shall remain anonymous, planted a fake bomb in one of the classrooms. No doubt, it was intended as a joke, but the school officials reacted quite seriously. Mr. Thomas called an assembly in the auditorium and characterized the incident as a "bomb scare" and emphasized that it was crime. His demeanor that day was anything but jovial.

Apparently, manipulation of the school bell system was a recurrent problem involving the Tandy boys. John's younger brother Bill Tandy (WSHS, 1964) also reset the timer causing an early dismissal of classes. This time it sufficiently peeved Mr. Thomas that he expelled Bill and required an appearance of his father, Captain John Tandy, the commanding officer of Highway Patrol Troop G, before Bill would be readmitted. I can't imagine the Tandy boys' older sister, the ever-pleasant Helen, committing an infraction of school rules.

Sandy (Merrill) Grogan told me of another cheerleading incident, which I had not heard about, that provoked his ire. Sandy said, "Between our junior and senior year, we decided that we just must have pom poms. Peggy [Henry] brought a magazine to practice that had an ad for just the ones we wanted. They were pretty expensive and a school administrator had to sign the order."

Obtaining the required signature created a logistical problem. As to how they overcame it, Sandy said, "Well, it was summer so we signed Mr. Thomas's name and planned to raise the money and have it for him when the merchandise arrived."

After the pompoms arrived, he summoned the senior cheerleaders into his office. Sandy says, "He was livid. I told him twice that I had worked hours and hours to pay for uniforms and the players didn't even have to buy their shoes. Furthermore, we would gladly send them back and wear regular school clothes to ballgames in the future. He calmed down as I got worked up. He said take the pom poms with us and make plans to pay for them." But according to Sandy, that was the last they heard about the matter.

While playing football my senior year, I sustained a major knee injury that required surgery in Springfield. In the operating room, a nurse remarked that I was from Willow Springs and asked if I knew Mr. Thomas. I told her that I did, and she said, "I'll bet he is a pretty mean guy." And I said, "Oh, no. I like Mr. Thomas." She said, "That's good, because he's my father." For the record, the nurse was his daughter Wanda. At the time, I was not aware he had a daughter, other than Sharon (WSHS, 1961).

Paraphrasing a description of Professor Dumbledore from Harry Potter, Fred Thomas was not proud or vain and could find value in every student, and enriched our lives.

"Fulltime" Phelps and the
Missouri Senate Showdown—Part 1

ONE OF THE MORE interesting jobs I've ever had, and certainly one of the most educational, was working for the Missouri Senate in 1973, as the reading clerk. That year, the upper house of the Missouri General Assembly provided political fireworks, and I got to be an eyewitness to history.

The 1972 election ushered in a number of "firsts." Christopher S. "Kit" Bond, inaugurated in 1973, became the first Republican governor since Forest C. Donnell in 1941, as well as the youngest governor in Missouri history. And on his coattails, a state representative from Kansas City, William C. "Bill" Phelps, became the first Republican lieutenant governor, since Edward Henry Winter in 1929. Phelps, while campaigning for the office, claimed he would make the lieutenant governor's office a full-time position, and he was quickly dubbed "Fulltime" Phelps.

More firsts happened closer to home, with the 1973 legislative term. Willow's favorite son, Wendell Bailey, began the first of his four terms as a state representative, and the quotable newspaperman/lawyer from Barry County, Emory Melton, secured the first of his six terms in the Missouri Senate.

Senator Melton often made me smile with the wry humor and wisdom he brought to the senate chamber with his Ozark quips. Once, in responding to a senator from Kansas City who sponsored a bill that could impact Emory's home district, he said, "In Barry County, we have heard of Kansas City, but in Kansas City, they have no idea where Barry County is."

The previous summer, before I ever met Senator Melton, I handed out election flyers for him at the request of Russell Corn, who had served as the state representative for Howell County from 1947 to 1962 and also as Willow Springs mayor. I was distributing campaign literature for Wendell Bailey, when Mr. Corn rushed out of his grocery store on First Street, and insisted that I also hand out pamphlets for his "good friend" Emory.

Essentially, the job of the senate reading clerk is to read bills out loud in the senate chamber. As part of the legislative process, some bills are required by law to be read in-full and others by title only. Any amendments offered by senators from the floor must be read in detail, loudly enough for all the senators to hear. I felt a bit like the town crier from colonial days.

As part of the interview process to get the job, I had to demonstrate the ability to project my voice while Venita Ramsey, the secretary of the senate, stood at the back of the senate chambers and listened. She apparently concluded my voice carried well enough. Hog calling from my Shannon County days and speech training from Mr. Newby at WSHS served me well.

Amendments from the floor could be entertaining. On a preprinted slip of paper, a senator would write the proposed change to a bill in longhand and signal for one of the ever-alert pages to deliver it to the Secretary, who would then hand it to me to read. I got so familiar with the various senators' penmanship that I could have been an authenticating witness in court.

In particular, I recall the flowery scroll of Earl Blackwell from Jefferson County. If you ever see a statute from that era that contains the language "all of the laws of the State of Missouri to the contrary notwithstanding," I'll wager it is Senator Blackwell's handiwork.

After the 1972 election, in addition to the offices of governor and lieutenant governor, the Republicans held significant power in the executive branch, with John Danforth as the attorney general and John Ashcroft as auditor. But the Democrats firmly controlled the Missouri Senate, by a margin of 21 to 13. And against this backdrop, a political firestorm smoldered.

The Missouri Constitution has two provisions that are key to this conflict. Pursuant to Article IV, Section 10, the lieutenant governor is president of the senate—in other words, the presiding officer. But Article 3, Section 18 grants the senate the right to determine its procedural rules. With the Democrats in the majority, the senate approved Rule 11 that allowed the president tempore (a democrat) to assume the chair at will.

In spite of the potential for conflict, business in the senate seemed to function in the usual course. Each day, Lieutenant Governor Phelps presided atop the large dais at the front of the senate chamber. At the lower level of the dais, Venita Ramsey,

several other clerks, and I sat within arm's length of the lieutenant governor. I often engaged in friendly conversation with
him, before the day's session started. He always seemed jovial,
particularly, if one of the clerks brought homemade cookies
to share.

The Missouri Senate Chamber. *Photo credit www.senate.mo.gov.*

But all the conviviality disappeared on June 15, 1973, the last
day of the legislative term. The last day of the session in both
houses of the General Assembly is jampacked and hectic. While
during the early part of the term, matters seemed to proceed
at a leisurely pace with much of the activity taking place in
committees.

The last day, however, is a scramble, plotted with military
precision. The legislators are hard-pressed to complete their
business before midnight and the session ends. I even heard
stories about the clocks being turned back to squeeze in more

time. For the record, I never witnessed that, but my sources seemed sincere.

I have read numerous newspaper accounts of what transpired that day and none accord exactly with my memory of what happened, but here's how I remember the events.

That last morning, just before Lieutenant Governor Phelps called the senate to order, Senator Lawrence "Larry" Lee from St. Louis, the Democratic Majority Floor Leader, strolled from his center aisle seat on the back row of the chamber and proceeded up the stairs of the elevated dais where Lieutenant Governor Phelps stood behind the podium. From my seat at the lower level of the dais, I sat within earshot of Phelps and Lee.

The two men passed a few perfunctory pleasantries, and Senator Lee handed the lieutenant governor a list of specified bills that were to be taken up, with the names of the senators to be recognized who were handling them, and then returned to his seat.

Phelps gaveled the chamber to order. Two senators stood to be recognized—a Democrat and Paul Bradshaw, a Republican from Springfield. Phelps recognized "the senator from Green County" who proceeded to take up a bill favored by the Republicans. Not calling on the senators that Democrats wanted had been a recurrent source of annoyance to the Democratic leadership.

William Cason, the president pro tempore, shot a hard glance at Larry Lee, and Senator Lee rushed down the aisle and up the steps of the dais to the upper level. "Governor, you're not following the list." Phelps replied, "Go sit down, senator."

"Fulltime" Phelps and the
Missouri Senate Showdown—Part 2

PART 1 FOCUSED ON the conflict that existed in the Missouri Senate in 1973 stemming from provisions of the Missouri Constitution. On one hand, the Constitution provided that the lieutenant governor was the presiding officer of the senate, but on the other, granted the senate rule-making authority.

On the surface the two provisions may not seem to be problematic, but when politics are involved, matters often become entangled. In 1973, the Democrats controlled the Missouri Senate by a margin of 21 to 13, and with the power to make procedural rules, the senate approved Rule 11, which allowed the president pro tempore (a democrat) to assume the position of presiding officer at will.

So, what's the big deal? It is the presiding officer in the senate who recognizes a particular senator to bring up a bill for voting, and the Democrats feared a Republican lieutenant governor would recognize a fellow Republican to take up a Republican-favored bill.

And that's what happened on the last day of the legislative session. Lieutenant Governor Phelps, not following the script the majority floor leader Larry Lee had given him, recognized Springfield Republican, Paul Bradshaw. And when Senator Lee hustled to the podium to correct the situation, Phelps told him to return to his seat.

But Senator Lee did not return to his seat. He made a beeline to the President Pro Tempore William Cason's desk. After some murmuring between the two senators, Senator Cason strode up the stairs of the dais and stood next to Phelps, and indicated he was assuming the chair under Senate Rule 11."

I don't remember the exact words of the conversation between Phelps and Cason, but the lieutenant governor asserted his constitutional right and refused to give up the podium.

Cason left the podium and headed to the entrance of the chamber where the sergeant at arms, James "Jimmy" Dunnavant, stood. Dunnavant, a Jefferson City police officer, although not tall, according to one Capitol news reporter, was tough. Moreover, he wore a holster with a pistol. Until that day, from my perspective, Jimmy just seemed to be a friendly, easy going fellow. Once, while talking to me about playing the guitar, he told me that country music star Little Jimmy Dickens tried to hire him for his band.

But after Senator Cason whispered in his ear, he marched forward and confronted Lieutenant Governor Phelps behind the podium. In a measured tone, Jimmy advised the lieutenant governor that he had to step down. Phelps refused.

By this time, I had turned around in my chair with my neck craned upwards, gawking at the spectacle taking place. Jimmy secured the lieutenant governor by the arm to "escort" him off the dais, but Phelps stood firm. Jimmy began pushing Phelps and maneuvering him down the steps toward the back door of the senate, with Phelps protesting in a loud voice.

The *Springfield Leader Press* reported his words as "I object, I object. I am president of the senate and this denies my constitutional right to preside." The *Kansas City Times* said, "Dunnavant . . . dragged the lieutenant governor, who was shouting that his constitutional rights and the rights of the people were being denied." A wire service indicated Phelps had "yelled and stomped his feet."

A few weeks later in a subsequent *Times* article, Phelps denied yelling or stomping his feet, and of his ejection, said, "I said in a very firm tone—I did not yell—that I had a constitutional right to the chair. Well, I said that all the way as I was pushed out of the chamber."

The variation in the reporting reminds me a bit of the "telephone" game where players in a line repeat a message to the person next to them. By the time the message reaches the person at the end of the line, it bears little resemblance to the original message.

From my ringside seat, Jimmy Dunnavant did not drag the lieutenant governor, nor was he "wrestled" out as the *Kansas City Times* headline indicated. Jimmy pushed him toward the back door in a real-life example of Isaac Newton's First Law of Motion, which some WSHS students might recall from teacher Neil Pamperien's physics class. Namely, that an object stays in place until acted upon by net force. In this instance, five-foot-something Jimmy pushing six-foot-plus Phelps, who added friction to the equation by bracing against him.

I almost couldn't believe what I was witnessing. It was like a bouncer in a barroom tossing a patron who didn't want to leave at closing time. After Phelps was ejected, an eerie silence ensued in the chamber. No whispering or murmurs. It was as if everybody quit breathing. Senators looked at each other. Reporters at the press table scribbled furiously. Then suddenly, all 13

William C. "Bill" Phelps, Lieutenant Governor of Missouri (1973-1981). *Photo credit: State of Missouri— Official Manual of the State of Missouri.*

Republican Senators stood up and marched out of the chamber in protest. And in short order, Cason and/or Lee directed the doorkeepers to lock the doors.

Phelps later tried to reenter the chambers but was prevented. He told the *Kansas City Times*, "When I approached the dais and attempted to take the chair, I was physically blocked by the sergeant-at-arms."

The *Springfield Leader Press* reported: "An angered Senate Minority Leader, A. Clifford Jones, R-Brentwood, told the senators their action was 'childish' and urged them to restore Phelps to the chair." When that didn't happen, the lieutenant governor sought relief from the Missouri Supreme Court.

At 3:30 P.M. that afternoon, Lieutenant Governor Phelps, represented by Attorney General John Danforth's office, filed a petition for a writ of prohibition (a court order) to "prevent Senator Cason, as President Pro Tempore, from interfering with the right of the Lieutenant Governor to preside over sessions of the Senate."

Unfortunately for the lieutenant governor, the Court denied the petition ". . . because the Court cannot in this limited time give to these issues the consideration warranted for final decision on the merits." As a result, Senator Cason or his designee presided over the senate until adjournment at midnight.

A final adjudication came on November 30, 1973. In *State of Missouri v. Cason*, the Missouri Supreme Court ruled that the Missouri Constitution's specific designation of the lieutenant governor as the presiding office of the senate trumped the rule-making authority granted to the senate. The Court recognized the Senate's right to make rules, but held, ". . . it may not by rule dilute the constitutional authority conferred on the lieutenant governor by Article IV, § 10."

The 1973 Missouri Senate showdown may have been a prime example of the cliché comparing laws and sausages—it's better not seeing them made. But 19th century author and philosopher Henry David Thoreau may have described it best. "Politics is, as it were, the gizzard of society, full of grit and gravel, and the two political parties are its opposite halves . . . which grind on each other."

Home Again

AUTHOR THOMAS WOLFE CLAIMED you can't go home again, and singer-songwriter Steve Earle crooning "Hometown Blues" wishes he had never returned home, because none of his old friends hung around there anymore. Well, that wasn't my experience retuning to Willow Springs on Memorial Weekend for the alumni reunion and a book-signing event for my second novel.

Our town has changed since the 1960s, when Willow was still larger than Licking and Mountain View, and had more than a half-dozen grocery stores, three clothing stores, two drugstores with pharmacists, three hardware stores, four automobile dealerships (Ford, Pontiac, Chrysler, and Chevrolet), three medical doctors, one dentist, a chiropractor, three taverns, a theater that showed movies, and no lawyers.

But each time I cruise into town, in my mind's eye, I can still see the buildings as they used to be and fondly remember people who populated them, such as butchers Phil Kilpatric (Wilbanks and later G&W) and Claude Bolerjack (Masoner's and later the Farmers' Exchange); Pharmacists Frank Protiva (Peoples Drugs) and Tommy Ferguson (Ferguson Drugs); and when Ferguson Drugs comes to mind, I always remember Sadie Ruth Ferguson, and the made-from-scratch limeade she conjured up from simple syrup and fresh limes.

The Montier Train Station, circa 1910, when Montier was a thriving whistle-stop town on the Frisco Railroad. The depot no longer exists. In the background of the photo, Silas Nicholson's general store can be seen. *Photo: public domain.*

My weekend trip included a jaunt to Montier on Friday to visit the cemetery and decorate family graves. Montier, named after a Frisco Railway official, was originally located a mile south of present U.S. Highway 60 in Shannon County, halfway between Mountain View and Birch Tree. Historically, it was a whistle-stop on the Current River Branch of Frisco Railroad.

With growth of the automobile, the town moved north of the cemetery to what is now old Highway 60. This was the Montier of the 1950s that I remember. It had a post office, a two-room school, two general stores (one owned by the parents of Willow residents Jo Anne Taylor and Janie Webb), and two churches, a

Methodist and a Church of God of Prophesy. Other than a small scattering of houses, only the Longnecker store building and the two churches remain, and the Methodist Church has been converted to a residence.

I have visited the Montier Cemetery numerous times and contributed to the caretaking fund managed by two generations of the Chowning family, but I never took flowers. This time it seemed appropriate, and I was moved beyond my expectations.

My maternal grandparents, Riley and Beulah Casey, are buried next to my great grandparents, Bill and Dema Casey. My great grandparents died before I was born, but stories I heard about them flashed in my mind as I placed the flowers on their sites.

According to family lore, Great Grandpa Bill, a former sheriff in Shannon County, arrested an outlaw from a notorious criminal gang in the 1930s, but the newspaper credit went to another law enforcement officer. Seeing the name Dema engraved in the headstone, I recalled discovering in the genealogy section of a library in Dallas, Texas, that she was actually named Susan Lodema. With that information, I deduced how my mother's sister Lodema got her name.

A weathered, flat gravestone lies next to Bill and Dema that bears the name Lillian I. Casey, my grandfather's youngest sister, and his favorite. Born in 1904, she died in her early 20s. I've only seen one photo of her, as a teenager, and it depicted a pretty girl full of life and playful.

My grandparents claimed she married a ne'er-do-well who took her to Oklahoma where she mysteriously died. An insurance policy may have been a motive. The husband, whose name is lost to history, arranged to return Lillian by train to Montier for burial. My grandfather waited at the Montier depot, with revenge on his mind. Her coffin arrived, but the husband had gotten off at an earlier stop and hightailed it out of the area.

The tragedy could have been compounded if the two men had met. My grandfather, a strapping blacksmith who worked on the Frisco section gang, might have been my great grandfather's next arrest. A sadness came over me as I reflected on the story, and I placed a single lily on Lillian's grave.

My maternal great, great grandfather, Riley H. McClellan, a Civil War veteran, is also buried there. As a child, I heard stories about some relative who had escaped from the Confederate prison at Andersonville, Georgia, but I never knew who it was. Several years ago, I read in "The History of Shannon County," published in 1986, that Riley H. McClellan had been imprisoned in Andersonville. I also learned he had three wives (at separate times) and thirteen children. It is a good thing that he escaped, or I wouldn't be writing this. I left a flower for him, too.

The escape story, as it was told to me, was he and another man charged past the "deadline," and Confederate guards started shooting. As they were running, Grandpa McClellan tripped and fell just before a bullet flew over his head. The guard yelled, "I got one of them." Grandpa jumped to his feet and yelled back at the guard, "You're a [expletive] liar."

The cemetery is well-maintained and looks much the same as ever. However, nothing else in Montier looks the same. Not from 60 years ago, and certainly, not from 100 years ago when Montier was a thriving whistle-stop on the Frisco line.

Late in the afternoon, I made it back to Willow and ventured out to my brother and sister-in-law's house. After their three German shepherds decided I wasn't a bandit, Sandy treated Jack and me to a delicious dinner of red beans and rice and strawberry shortcake.

Saturday kicked off, thanks to John Bailey, with the book signing at Bailey's Chevrolet. Without a doubt, it was my most fun book event ever, beginning with the early arrival and clarion call of Wendell Bailey, "I'm here to buy books." Jane Bailey arrived shortly thereafter and generously bought books to donate to the Willow Springs Library and the elementary school.

I felt genuinely honored by the folks who showed up. In particular, Amanda Mendez, the owner and publisher of the *Howell County News*, took time off from her maternity leave to drop by with new baby Joseph. And Debra Duddridge, whom I met via telephone a couple years ago when I was arranging a catering event, sent her husband James to Willow to get a book.

I would be remiss if I didn't mention classmates who came: Donna Spence Romans, Carol Hale Aldridge, Joe Corn (with wife Janie), and Buddy Stuart (with brothers, Charles and Mike). Friends from other classes included, Joan Hagener Ott, Alice Brook West, Beverly Hill Gray, Steve Losh, Billie Frye Thurman, and John Foster. After the crowd dwindled, I had an enjoyable time talking "shop" with writer Jill Bailey.

The alumni barbeque Saturday night marked an excellent recovery from the pandemic, and provided a marvelous opportunity to talk with more friends and meet a few new ones. Kudos to Tom and Phyliss White and volunteers for their hard work.

For me the weekend closed in the lobby of the Comfort Inn Saturday night with Barbara Sherrill Pig, Dee Collins Corn, Roberta Haase Donnell, and Charlie Hord laughing like teenagers, as we remembered the way we were.

Silas Nicholson's general store in "old" Montier as it appears today.

Blackberry Summer and the 4th of July

IN THE 1950S, THE summers seemed longer and hotter, and according to weather records some were definitely hotter, particularly in two brush-covered bottoms of the Shannon County farm of my grandparents. And that's where the wild blackberries grew.

Stupendous blackberries. Big ones, the size of a kid's thumb. Not the pitiful, scrawny ones growing in the dusty roadside ditches, but plump, juicy ones that thrived in the two five-acre depressions between hills of the mostly wooded farm. In years past, the bottoms were likely cultivated cornfields, but had been taken over by aggressive stands of sassafras and sumac that allowed just the right amount of sunlight for blackberries to prosper.

During blackberry season in late June and July, the entire family became pickers. Grandma made cobblers and jam and froze them. Her cobblers weren't the traditional type, baked with a crust on the top or bottom. She made her version on top of the wood-burning cookstove in a large sauce pan, and as the berries simmered, she dropped in baking powder dumplings.

She learned this method when she and Grandpa lived in a tent in the Oklahoma oil fields because using the oven made a hot tent unbearable.

Watching a TV cooking program a few years ago, I learned Grandma's concoction wasn't technically a cobbler but is called a "grunt," not to be confused with a "slump." A slump is also fruit confection cooked with yeast dumplings and not a baked crust, and is so-named because it has no defined shape when dumped on a plate. Similarly, a grunt has no baked crust, but has baking powder dumplings, and its name supposedly comes from the sound it makes as it cooks.

Stalking the wild blackberry (apologies to forager Euell Gibbons) required preparation. Regardless of the temperature, the brambles made long-sleeved shirts, jeans, and boots the required uniform. Blackberry season is the only time I ever saw my grandmother in pants. She owned one pair of blue dungarees reserved for blackberry picking.

Looking back, gloves might have been a good idea. After having my hands punctured and scratched by thorns, juice from the blackberries seeped in the scrapes making black tattoos that looked like scrimshaw inked by a drunken sailor that took days to wear off.

The sassafras jungle also created a perfect habitat for rabbits and mice, which meant you needed to be alert for copperheads. My grandmother claimed she could smell them in a briar patch. Maybe she could, but I never saw her demonstrate the skill.

The most offensive creatures in the woods—ticks—were abundant and relentless. We didn't have Backwoods Off, but for a repellant, we bushed our pantlegs and shirtsleeves with sprigs of pennyroyal, which we called "peppermint weed." (Now, you can buy "natural" tick and flea collars for pets made out of pennyroyal.) Any ticks that hitchhiked home with us got baptized with kerosene. Short of igniting it, I'm not sure the kerosene did much good. But I can't imagine the ticks liked it—I certainly did not.

Equipped with two 4-pound Krey lard buckets with wire bale handles strapped to our belts, my brother Jack and I headed out early to avoid the heat. It was amazing the number of berries we could collect. In a few hours, we'd return to the house with full buckets.

We got more than we needed for home use, and after we filled Grandma's requirements, we scouted other fields for berries and sold them at Welsh's Montier Grocery. With July 4th coming soon, we used our blackberry money to buy fireworks.

The Fourth of July celebration on the farm highlighted the summer. It meant homemade ice cream, made with cream from a Jersey cow, so thick it could be skimmed with a ladle. We hand-cranked the ice cream churn, an old wooden 5-gallon bucket with a steel cylinder inside full of cream, sugar, and vanilla, surrounded by ice and rock salt until the cream mixture froze. Of course, ice cream could have been purchased at the store, but with fresh blackberries on top, in my view, our homemade ice cream would lay Ben and Jerry's in the shade. Weeks prior to the Fourth, Jack saved his money and on the weekly trip to Mountain View carefully selected fireworks—the most exotic he could afford: Big Blasters, Star Bursts, and one that promised to finish with a parachute falling from the sky. He exercised patience and didn't explode any before the holiday, unlike his younger brother who mostly bought firecrackers and set them off as soon as he got home.

On the Fourth, Jack waited until darkness had fallen to set off his fireworks. And the display topped off the evening. His pyrotechnic devises functioned as advertised, including the parachuting soldier. My one contribution, a foot-tall skyrocket, which I had refrained from shooting off, did not soar into the heavens as I had imagined. Instead, it fizzled in a low trajectory over the road and crashed on Billy Barnes's property, prompting my grandfather's concern of a brush fire.

Jack did not outgrow his fireworks fascination with adulthood. Every year, in anticipation of a July 4th celebration on his farm, he stockpiled a bountiful supply of fireworks to put on a show for his kids, and later his grandkids.

But another fireworks exhibition involving my brother stands out in my mind. One 4th of July in the early 1970s (I recall because I was still in law school), I camped with Jack, Sandy, and the kids at Blue Springs on the Jacks Fork. Of course, Jack came supplied with fireworks, including bottle rockets. One thing led to another, and Jack and I established opposing battle stations and started launching bottle rockets at each other. [Public Service Announcement: Do not try this foolish, unsafe practice.]

Apparently, Jack's Marine Corps training led him to establish a superior position on higher ground. Nevertheless, I managed to dodge the incoming rockets and launch my own fair share until one of his rockets landed in my ammo dump igniting my rocket supply and causing me to scramble for cover. I waved the white flag of surrender and returned to peacetime activities.

Wrong Turn at Pismo Beach

IN THE 1950S, MY brother and I saw a Looney Tunes cartoon on TV featuring Bugs Bunny and Elmer Fudd. In the video, Elmer, wielding his trusty ("twusty," that is) double-barreled shotgun, chased the rascally rabbit until Bugs escaped by jumping down into his rabbit hole.

Bugs began burrowing furiously, and in the next several frames visible from a distant view, his burrowing trail could be seen going around the Earth. Then, in a closeup shot, Bugs sticks his head out of his burrow and is surround by Asian-looking people wearing conical-shaped hats, and says, "I must have taken a wrong turn at Pismo Beach."

At the time, I had no idea that Pismo Beach was a real place in California, but years later "a wrong turn at Pismo Beach" became my catchphrase for every mistake I made. If an event didn't turn out as I expected—I must have made a wrong turn at Pismo Beach. But in the summer of 1967, it was a wrong turn at Miami Beach that caused problems for me.

Although my family lived in Willow Springs in the 1960s, 600 miles from the nearest seaport, my stepfather, George Rothwell, earned a living as a merchant seaman. It wasn't unusual for him to be gone for three to six months a year traveling to exotic countries like India or Egypt.

After each trip, he returned home with exciting tales of casbahs and strange food. He often brought jewelry, crafted by foreign artisans, to my mother. For me, it was always a foreign language newspaper that appeared to be written in gibberish, which I couldn't read. His trips, nevertheless, sounded glamorous to me—I suspect it wasn't.

In 1967, with George's planning and direction, I was on track to acquire a merchant seaman's license and have my own seafaring adventure. The amount of money I would earn as a deck hand on a merchant vessel would pay for a year of college.

Obtaining a merchant seaman's certificate, which allowed one to depart the country and work on a merchant ship, came with a few hurtles to clear. As prerequisite to applying, someone with my lack of knowledge, skill, or nautical ability needed a letter from a merchant marine shipping company stating my services were needed.

After sailing multiple times for a particular company, George managed to get the company to issue the required letter. With my letter in hand, I traveled to the Coast Guard office in St. Louis to apply for a merchant seaman's certificate. In addition to the application form, I had to sign a lengthy document, under the penalty of perjury, that I had never been a member of the Communist Party or scores of other subversive organizations listed on the form, few of which I recognized.

Because the whole process seemed so official, it concerned me a bit that I might have missed some group on the subversive organization list, and FBI agents might track me down later. The issuing coast guard official added to my angst telling me how hard it was to obtain a merchant seaman's card and that I should guard it carefully.

George Rothwell (L) with a shipmate at an Indian port, circa 1968.

Just because I had a license didn't ensure that I would get assigned to a ship. My mother told me George had arranged for a case of Cutty Sark scotch to be delivered to a certain port official in Houston, Texas, to get me aboard a ship.

According to the plan, when I finished my sophomore year at Mizzou, I was to fly to Houston, Texas, rent a sleeping room, and then go to the seaman's union hall and ask for a Mr. "Jones," who would get me on a ship. It was a reasonable plan . . . until I made a route deviation.

Shortly, before heading to Texas, I had a conversation with my freshman year dormitory roommate, Lynn Spence (WSHS, 1964). Lynn had moved to Florida to pursue a career in aviation, and on semester break, I flew to Miami to visit him. In those days, flying standby with a student discount was relatively cheap, and with a free place to stay, it was an affordable trip.

During our conversation, Lynn suggested it would be a good time to visit Florida again and hangout with him and the new friends I had met that spring. A tempting offer indeed, but I explained my funds were limited, and that I only had enough money to fly to Houston.

If Lynn hadn't become a pilot, he would have been excellent in sales. In fact, he won the title of *Willamizzou* Supersalesman as a senior. Always logical and persuasive, he suggested if I had enough money to fly to Houston that I had enough to fly to Florida, and that he would loan me the money to fly from Miami to Houston. Moreover, I could pay him back at the end of the summer from all the money I would make as a merchant seaman.

I agreed to fly to Florida. After all, I reasoned, what could a few days hurt? I never advised my mother of this change of plans. As far as she knew, when I left Willow, I was on my way to Texas. George was on voyage to India, so he was unaware.

Initially, my sojourn to Florida proved to be as much fun as my previous visit, sightseeing and swimming in the ocean, until my absentmindedness crashed the party. Returning from the beach one evening with Lynn and other friends, I realized my billfold was missing, with all my money—and my merchant seaman's card.

To this day, I cringe when I recall the sinking feeling that hit me. A feeling of abject fear. What would I tell my mother and George?

I must have taken a wrong turn at Pismo (Miami) Beach.

Home from Pismo Beach

THE PREVIOUS ARTICLE, "WRONG Turn at Pismo Beach," ended with losing my merchant seaman's license on the beach in Miami, Florida, when I was supposed to be in Houston, Texas.

To recap, in 1967, the summer after my sophomore year at Mizzou, my stepfather had arranged for me to acquire a merchant seaman's license and get aboard a ship out of Houston. Instead of going directly to Houston, I detoured to Florida to visit my former roommate, Lynn Spence, and ended up losing my wallet, money, and seaman's license on the beach.

The next morning Lynn and I returned to the beach administrative office to check the lost and found department. Surprisingly, a good Samaritan had turned in my wallet, with no money inside, but, amazingly, it still contained my merchant seaman's license.

Lynn, true to his word, loaned me money for a plane ticket to Houston, and a little extra to tide me over until my ship came in.

I landed in Houston, clueless as to how to get to the water-front. A map on the wall informed me it was too far to walk.

After asking for directions, I hoisted my seabag on my shoulder, found a bus stop, and headed for the waterfront. In an hour or so, I stood in front of the Harrisburg Hotel, a place my stepfather regularly stayed.

The Harrisburg Hotel would never appear on a Houston tourist brochure. It had been converted from a two-story house to a sleeping room establishment. A hand-painted sign above the front door announced, "Rooms, $1.99 for 24 hours." I forked over two bucks, and the desk clerk showed me a room on the second floor and pointed to the communal bathroom a few doors down the hall.

The room matched its low rent, with a bare wooden floor, peeling wallpaper, a sagging bed in an iron frame, and a single light bulb hanging from the ceiling by an electrical cord. A wooden chest of drawers provided the only other amenity.

My first night, a group of hoodlum-looking young men, who loitered in the vacant lot across the street, hauled the soda machine from the lobby over to "their" lot and robbed it. Apparently not satisfied, they broke into the room next to mine. I never heard a thing. The clerk told me about it the next morning, and the soda machine was still in the lot across the street.

After a cheap breakfast, I headed to the seaman's union hall and found "Mr. Jones." He motioned me into his office. He did not look like a happy man. "Where have you been?" he asked. "You were supposed to be here last week." He continued speaking over my attempted explanation. "There's a longshoremen's strike going on. I could have gotten you on a ship last week. Now, nothing's going out."

Mr. Jones told me the only thing I could do was try to wait it out. For nearly a week, I hung out at the union hall, waiting and playing cards with the landlocked sailors. But the strike never ended before I ran out of money. I had no choice but to get back home.

At the time, credit cards were virtually unknown. All I had was my checkbook for the Bank of Willow Springs. I called my brother, and he agreed to put some money in my account, but I still needed to get an out-of-state personal check cashed. Several blocks away, I found the Harrisburg Bank and told the teller I wanted to cash a check drawn on the Bank of Willow Springs. My request exceeded her authority, and she directed me to the vice president's office.

I explained my situation to the vice president. He did not seem impressed. In fact, he seemed suspicious. My only identification was a merchant seaman's card and a check from some small town in Missouri. He warned me about the penalties for writing a bad check, but he agreed to call the Willow Springs Bank. I told him to ask for Joyce Burns or Eddie Ogden, Jr. I felt sure either would vouch that I was not a crook. One benefit of growing up in a small town is you know the town fathers, including the bankers. And with bankers Joyce Burns and Eddie Ogden, their children were my schoolmates.

Since this was also before telephone direct-dialing, he had his secretary contact the operator to get the number and place a long-distance call. Only in small town in the Ozarks in the 1960s could this happen—the bank's number was busy. For whatever reason, perhaps because my story was too strange to have been concocted, he agreed to cash my check without placing another call.

I flew standby to St. Louis and made my way to the bus station downtown and bought a ticket to Rolla. After midnight, I got off the bus at the Rolla bus depot. Within minutes, a Rolla policeman approached and began questioning me. He told me to get into his cruiser, and then drove south to the city limits on Highway 63 and told me to get out.

In the early morning hours traffic was sparce, and the drivers who passed by ignored my extended thumb. Around 2 a.m., a man driving a truck with stock racks stopped and asked me where I was going. When I told him, he said, "Get in. I'm headed to West Plains." The truck bed was empty. He was returning from delivering a load of hogs to Chicago. I could have guessed that from the smell that still lingered. Nevertheless, I felt fortunate.

Sometime after sunrise, he stopped his truck in front of my house on High Street. My visibly annoyed mother met me at the door. I don't remember the conversation, but I still remember how she looked. And one thing I knew for sure, I needed to find a summer job.

My buddy Royce Yardley (WSHS, 1966) was in town, and we made a pact that we would work together hauling hay and doing other manual labor jobs. I envisioned a long, boring summer, but within a few days, I received an unsolicited phone call from a director of the St. Louis Area Boy Scouts. He wanted to know if I had a Red Cross Water Safety Instructor's license. When I told him I did, he offered me a job as the waterfront director at Beaumont Scout Reservation in rural St. Louis County.

I agreed to accept the job, provided he would also hire Royce as a lifeguard. Royce had a Red Cross Senior Lifesaving certification. Sight unseen, on the basis of a telephone inter-view and my recommendation of Royce, he hired us both for the summer.

So, my wrong turn at Pismo Beach had a happy ending. Royce and I spent an interesting summer teaching swimming and lifesaving lessons at Beaumont Scout Reservation. But to this day, I regret missing my great sea adventure. Oh, the stories I could have told.

Summer Camps

EVER SINCE SEEING HAILEY Mills in the original movie Parent Trap, I've had a whimsical attraction to summer camps. It wasn't just an eighth-grade infatuation with a teenage movie star; I liked the whole ambience of distant wooded areas, lakes, campfires, and swimming, And, as I have written before, a Red Cross Water Safety Instructor Certification (WSI) enabled me to work at several summer camps.

Like many things, my first knowledge of a WSI started in Willow Springs. In the early 1960s, teacher Buddy Bennett coached high school baseball and all junior high sports. One summer he coached the youth baseball programs in Willow, but most summers, because he had a WSI, he worked as the waterfront director at Camp Wakonda, a privately owned camp on the Lake of the Ozarks.

I recall he had a nifty WSI patch on his swimming trunks, which I viewed as a formidable badge of distinction. He told cool stories about campfire programs, lifeguarding, and watermelon fights, where campers and staff would pummel each other with hunks of watermelon, in good-natured fun. I suppose, no pun intended, a proverbial seed was planted in my mind.

College student volunteers at White Oak Camp for underprivileged children located at Hammond Mill near Dora, Missouri, in August 1966. From (L) to (R): Lonnie Whitaker, swimming instructor; Gary Evan, counselor; Mike Warning, counselor; Deanna Collins, counselor; and Joe Corn, lifeguard. *Photo courtesy of Deanna Collins Corn.*

The lifeguarding path for me and a couple schoolmates, Joe Corn (WSHS, 1965) and Royce Yardley (WSHS, 1966), started in Willow at Smokey Stover's swimming pool. Smokey owned a motel on Main Street located approximately where the Sonic is today, and, in the early 1960s, he constructed an indoor pool adjacent to it.

To describe it as an indoor pool is a bit of a stretch. In actual fact, it was an outdoor pool housed inside aqua-and yellow-colored, corrugated fiberglass walls and a roof, and during the summer it got quite steamy inside. Nevertheless, it is where the three of us obtained our junior and senior Red Cross lifesaving badges, which provided the prerequisites for a WSI.

Judy Scott (basketball coach Joe Scott's wife) instructed us in junior lifesaving, and local resident Alice Perkins trained us in the senior course. A girl from Alton, an athletic, strong swimmer, drove to Willow to take the senior training. I recall her well, since she nearly drowned me in one of the exercises, but I finally managed to escape her choke hold. Lesson learned: duck your chin when attacked from behind.

When I started college, Mizzou required students to take physical education classes twice a week. However, WSI certification training, which was considerably more challenging, could be substituted for PE. I signed up and passed the course, which opened several doors of opportunity for me in 1966.

That summer, with a newly-acquired WSI, I got a job as the waterfront director at Camp Clover Point, a 4-H camp on the Lake of the Ozarks near Kaiser, Missouri, five miles south of the Grand Glaze Bridge.

The 4-H campers, mostly small town and farm kids, all seemed appreciative and happy to be at the rustic setting of a former Civilian Conservation Corps (CCC) camp that offered few amenities. I don't recall a whiner in the bunch. Perhaps a week not driving a tractor or assisting with canning chores provided a welcomed break.

I've taught swimming in fancier places such as the Beaumont Scout Reservation in St. Louis County, mentioned in my last article, or teaching university students for a couple semesters at Mizzou. But it never felt as rewarding as working with the kids at Clover Point, or later that summer, at White Oak Camp at Hammond Mill in Ozark County.

The Missouri Extension Service sponsored both Camp Clover Point and White Oak Camp. After Clover Point closed for the summer, Gilbert Rader, the area Missouri Extension agent and director of White Oak Camp, hired me as the swimming instructor. Willow Springs schoolmates of mine, Deanna Collins (WSHS, 1964), Mike Warning (WSHS, 1964), and Gary Evans (WSHS, 1964) had already been hired as camp counselors, and classmate Joe Corn (WSHS, 1965) was onboard as a lifeguard.

Located at the former CCC camp at Hammond Mill southeast of Dora, Missouri, White Oak Camp was specifically designated for local underprivileged kids. The quality of life they came from surprised some of the volunteers. Recalling her experience as a counselor there, Deanna Collins Corn recently told me, "The only thing that is still so vivid to me is how many of the kids came to camp with nothing. No change of clothes, no swim suit, no toothbrush or toothpaste, no brush or comb, no pj's, etc."

The gratitude the kids showed for the slightest acknowledgment or attention motivated us to made their experience positive. Deanna says, "After that first week and the shock of these needy kids, I told my mom that I needed to gather clothing, brushes/combs, toothbrushes, and toothpaste . . . I thought I understood being poor, but these kids were in another level of doing without necessities."

Deanna also understood their need for personal attention. She says, "I know that second week I spent our free time brushing hair and helping the 8-year-old girls place their hair in ponytails and pigtails. I took hair ribbons and hair fasteners and the girls were so excited. It was a major influence on my life's work." [Deanna became a successful teacher and school administrator. No doubt, the campers adored the pretty college woman who pampered and encouraged them.]

Our first priority as staff members was to keep the campers safe, but a big part of our jobs was to make sure they had fun, and swimming played a big part. The old CCC camp didn't have a swimming pool, and it is doubtful many of the kids had ever been in one, but the nearby North Fork River served quite well.

Several times a day, lifeguard Joe Corn and I transported the kids to the creek in an old school bus. Joe says of those trips, "The bus was old, with a 4-speed on the floor and poor brakes. There was a hill we traveled to the swimming hole, and we were very careful to gear down going downhill and keep the speed slow."

Joe recalled that the swimming area "was an old abandoned concrete low-water crossing with a fairly shallow swim area. Downstream was the new overhead bridge. It was close to the Twin Bridges recreation canoe facility." We did little swimming instruction, although most the kids could have used lessons. We just lifeguarded and let them have fun.

One memory from the White Oak Camp at Hammond Mill that has endured for me stems from the bus trips to the creek. Because the bus was yellow, all the way there and back, Joe and I led the kids in singing the Beatles song, "Yellow Submarine." The singing by those kids might better be described as enthusiastic yelling, but I've never heard but a more joyful sound.

A Pirate Retrospective

WITH THE COMING OF fall, my mind returns to Howell County football of the 1960s. Although I am a Willow Bear, with scars earned over six years on Palenske Field, I don't mind tipping my hat to some of the players and teams from the eastern part of the county.

Before the Liberty Eagles, the Pirates ruled the roost in Mountain View. In the late fifties and early sixties, under the leadership of Coach Bud Glazier and Assistant Coach Dan Atha, Mountain View produced some outstanding football players and an SCA Conference co-championship team in 1960.

Mountain View added football to its athletic curriculum in 1948, when members of that championship team were, as put by the Mountain View Standard, "first-graders at the time." For many older Pirate fans, however, it was Coach Bud Glazer who changed the football landscape in Mountain View.

In fact, Glazier literally changed the landscape. During his tenure, a new football field (the present one used by the Liberty Eagles) can be credited among Coach Glazier's accomplishments.

Previously, the Pirates played on the baseball field on the eastern edge of town. Bill Webb (MVHS, 1963) says, "We played on the new field at the beginning of the 1959 season. Bud Glazier, with some other school employees, did much of the work on it themselves."

I remember playing on that field in 1959 when my junior high team lost to Mountain View 20-14. The 1½-inch Zosia grass had turned yellow, but provided more cushioning than the rocky top field behind the elementary school (now, behind Munford's Gym) where we practiced. I wasn't the only one impressed. Of the new field, an official from Springfield said, "They've got the finest football field—grass and lights—I've seen in Southwest Missouri."

Prior to coaching at Mountain View, Coach Glazier played high school football at Mountain Grove and college football at Wichita University and Southwest Missouri State and coached at Midway High School in Stark City, Missouri. After five years at Mountain View, he became head football coach at Rolla High School for two years, and in 1964 was named assistant coach at the Missouri School of Mines. Later in his career, he coached and became a principal at Salem High School.

Even good coaches need good players for success, and Mountain View had a bunch. When I first moved to Willow, my buddy Truman Grogan told me about Pirate speedsters Davis Roush and Kenneth Pennycuick—two names often referred to in tandem. Roush earned first-team all-SCA and all-Ozark honorable mention as quarterback his junior year in 1958, and, remarkably, grabbed first-team all-conference and second-team all-Ozark honors the next year as a halfback.

The 1960 championship season produced a boatload of individual awards. Quarterback Howard Henry and linemen Butch Gray, Tom McLaughlin, and Don Abbey achieved first-team all-conference status. Howard Henry also received honorable mention all-Ozark. Second-team all-SCA distinction went to Glenn Miller, Tom Howe, and Junior Barnum. Kent Depee and Mike Butler received SCA honorable mention.

Lineman Butch Gray, a Pirate legend, led the 1960 team in postseason honors earning first-team all-Ozark and all-state honorable mention.

Teammate Bill Webb recalls, "Butch Gray transferred in that year, and he probably had more athletic ability than Mountain View had ever seen from a high school athlete up until then. Butch played guard on offense and middle linebacker on defense and was a game changer." Years later, a knowledgeable source told me an essential part of the Pirate game plan in a memorable victory over West Plains was Butch Gray tackling Zizzer all-Ozark running back John Findley.

The next few years Mountain View did not achieve the team success of the 1960 season, but nevertheless, continued to produce quality players. Center Tom McLaughlin, voted SCA Lineman of the Year in 1961, notched a spot on the all-Ozark second team in 1961 and 1962. Bill Webb, after racking up a bunch of receiving yards as an end, received honorable mention all-Ozark and made the all-conference second team in 1962. Quarterback Kent Depee received second-team all-conference honors in 1962.

Although Willow Springs and Mountain View weren't arch rivals, the relationship was competitive. In the 1962 season,

Willow played Mountain View twice, and in the second match, a couple players demonstrated their competitive nature.

Did you ever wonder what type of skulduggery might take place at the bottom of a pile of players after a gang tackle? Stealing the ball? Biting? Gouging? All of the above? Or as one former Mountain View player told me of a particular incident, "I had a memorable meeting with one of your teammates."

The Mountain View player, "Smith," expanded on the memorable meeting. "I remember being tackled and was on the bottom of the pile, face down. One of my hands inadvertently ended up inside the faceguard of a Willow Springs player. Before I could move my hand away, this player started biting hard on one of my fingers. With the weight of the players on top of me, I couldn't move or use my other hand to defend myself."

Smith says he tried to use his "free fingers that he didn't have in his mouth" to scratch or poke the Willow player ("Jones") to make him release his fingers. "The pile broke up and the biter let go, but I didn't determine who he was."

At the time, Smith was dating a Willow girl and says, "On a date a few nights after the game, [she] asked me if I had been bitten by anyone during the game. I told her the story, and she said Jones proudly confessed to her that he did it. We both had a good laugh."

I had a good laugh, too, since I know Jones. Although the two haven't met since their encounter at the bottom of the pile, Smith says, "Despite his biting tendencies, I hear he is a good man." He added, "If you are still in touch with him, please tell him that he made an impression on me that I won't forget and that I wish him well."

I contacted Jones and inquired about his alleged "Hannibal Lecter" behavior and asked him to fess up or say it ain't so. Jones claimed his biting was purely defensive to keep from being poked in the eye. As to what actually happened, it appears to be a dogfall—an inconclusive result or a tie—like the Bear/Pirate record in 1962. The Pirates won the first match 20 to zip, and the Bears prevailed in the second game 20-13.

The identities of "Alias Smith and Jones" shall remain anonymous because both players are now esteemed citizens in their respective communities, and shenanigans of the past ought not cause them to be held up to contempt and ridicule or to be shunned and avoided. And for the record, I am not Jones.

In this article, I tried to be as inclusive as possible, but given the somewhat limited resources available to me, I no doubt failed to mention someone's favorite player or some important fact, but hope I have stirred fond memories of a bygone era of Mountain View football.

My thanks to Jeanne Sharp Gaddy for providing photos and to Alias Smith and Jones for inside information.

Lowell McMurtrey:
WSHS Alumnus, Teacher, and POW

MY FRESHMAN YEAR IN 1961, I heard the sophomores talk about how hard the new World History teacher was and how much homework he assigned. Some girls said they were afraid of him. One guy told me Mr. McMurtrey slammed a burly upper-classman against a locker for mouthing off.

Lowell McMurtrey projected a formidable presence in the classroom, but for me he proved to be an excellent teacher, and one not soon forgotten. Knowledgeable and interesting, he wanted students to think and not just parrot information.

In some respects, his teaching technique was that of a law school professor asking probing questions to engage a student's mind. Of a particular historic event, he would typically ask, "What's the significance of that?" On his tests, students got points for remembering the facts, but received additional credit for knowing why the fact was important.

But woe to the student not paying attention. A few years ago, classmate David Zimmerman recalled an incident when Mr.

McMurtrey caught Jimmy "Tee" Thomas (Class of '65 valedictorian) reading his math book during World History class. David said, "He took Jimmy's math book and threw it up against the back wall in history class. Tee jumped about 3-feet off his chair."

His likeable son Kenny was a classmate in World History. Mr. McMurtrey would matter of factly call on Kenny in class, without any indication of their relationship or recrimination for an incorrect answer. I don't recall anyone ever talking to Kenny about his dad. I never did. We were politely respectful like that back then.

Who was this teacher, who at times sparked controversy and had detractors, but also had students who claimed him as their best teacher ever? A deft summary, written by faculty editor Jessie Munford in the 1962 *Willamizzou*, provides some insight. "Alumnus Lowell McMurtrey finally came home to teach two classes of world history, one in citizenship, and a class in driver education." Additionally, she noted, "Mr. McMurtrey is a voluminous reader—three daily newspapers, numerous magazines, and historical books."

Without excessive sentimentality, Mrs. Munford succinctly added, "A veteran of World War II, who suffered months of imprisonment, he is an ardent advocate of democracy. His classes have appreciated a well-organized unit on world communism as well as the dangers of extreme rightists."

Other than yearbook copy describing a faculty member, what was Mrs. Munford's intent? Aware that people other than students read the *Willamizzou*, I suspect it was a rhetorical defense of Mr. McMurtrey.

Because he talked about totalitarian governments and communists in his classes, some parents concluded he was teaching communism and registered complaints. Marilyn Sherrill Cummins (WSHS, 1964) says, "I remember when Mr. McMurtrey was teaching us about communism and he almost lost his job. He wanted us to know about communism and what it does to people and the school board took it as if he was teaching us to be communists."

At the time, I thought the uproar was ridiculous, and Mrs. Munford, who obviously understood the object lesson of the Chicken Little story, wanted an accurate recording for posterity.

Rumors abounded about Mr. McMurtrey. We knew he had been a prisoner of war, but our information was vague. He, like most of his generation, didn't talk about his war experience. Some thought he had escaped from a Stalag and trudged under the cover of darkness from Germany to France. Some thought he had been on the Bataan Death March. So, what's the real Lowell McMurtrey story?

Lowell's father, McKinley (M.K.) McMurtrey, a lawyer admitted to practice in 1919, moved his wife and their only child to Willow Springs in 1938, after practicing law in Washington and Wright

Private Lowell McMurtrey in his U.S. Army uniform during World War II. *Courtesy of State Historical Society of Missouri from the Lowell and Margaret M. McMurtrey Papers 1942-1971 (C4172).*

Counties. In 1944, Governor Donnell appointed M.K. to the bench as Howell County Probate Judge.

Lowell, born in Potosi, Missouri, on August 24, 1922, graduated from WSHS in 1941. The '41 *Willamizzou* pictures a darkly handsome young man and the attribution, "Too bad girls, he's already attached." On June 11, 1942, he married Margaret Mitchell [not the author of Gone with the Wind], the daughter of Mr. and Mrs. Roy Mitchell of Willow Springs. [Some readers will recall Roy Mitchell operated a small grocery store at the corner of Walnut and Park where he held court when he was the Willow Springs police judge.]

After graduation he worked for a period at Garrett's Grocery and attended college at Arkansas State in Jonesboro. In December 1942, newly married and 20-years old, Lowell enlisted in the United States Army a year after the Japanese attack at Pearl Harbor.

I surmise from a local newspaper account that he left the day after Christmas for basic training at Fort Knox, Kentucky, home of the Armored Force School. There, Lowell and other recruits received training in the use of tanks and other armored vehicles.

Lowell never got a furlough home after basic training. The *Journal-Gazette*, a West Plains newspaper, reported, "When he [McMurtrey] had been in the army four months he went overseas to Africa. He went through the African campaign in the Seventh Army [commanded by General George S. Patton, Jr.] and was then transferred to the Fifth Army [commanded by General Mark Wayne Clark] and saw action at the Salerno landing." Some of the fiercest fighting of the war happened in Italy.

On March 1, 1944, the War Department, by telegram, notified his mother, Adel McMurtrey, that her son had been reported missing in action since February 3, 1944.

Later in life, Lowell and Margaret McMurtrey donated correspondence, photos, and newspaper clippings to the University of Missouri, which are stored at the State Historical Society in Columbia. I arranged for the collection to be couriered to the St. Louis Research Center on the UMSL campus. The files proved to be a treasure trove of information.

At the beginning of my research for this article, I pictured the 6-foot, solidly-built teacher I knew in the 1960s. A man who spoke with command authority and didn't suffer nonsense from students. But in the process my view changed. I recalled a course I took in which the instructor led the class in a meditation exercise. He asked us to visualize a scene from childhood. In my mind's eye, I saw my parents and was startled at how young they looked—younger than I was at the time. The exercise gave me a different perspective and appreciation of them.

Similarly, holding Mr. McMurtrey's dog tags and the War Department telegram reporting him missing in action, and reading the postcards of a young man, who only wanted to get home to his wife and parents, changed my understanding of Lowell McMurtrey.

I will share more in Part 2 of the Lowell McMurtrey story.

Mr. McMurtrey—Part 2

IN MY PREVIOUS ARTICLE, "Lowell McMurtrey, WSHS Alumnus, Teacher, and POW," I mentioned that researching newspaper accounts and the records preserved by the State Historical Society of Missouri gave me a different perspective of my former teacher. A more personal, human understanding, which I wanted to convey, and also provide an accurate account of what happened.

Lowell McMurtrey, a 1941 graduate of WSHS, entered the U.S. Army in December 1942, after marrying Margaret Mitchell just six months before. He received basic training as a tank cannoneer at Ft. Knox, Kentucky, and four months later was on ship bound for North Africa to join the 7th Army commanded by General George S. Patton, Jr.

Several of the newspapers of the day indicated that Mr. McMurtrey enlisted in the Army. Reading them I thought it odd or extremely patriotic that he would enlist after being married for only 6 months. Nevertheless, I included that information in Part 1. Since then, I obtained additional information from the

State Historical Society of Missouri (SHS) that indicated those newspaper reports may not have been accurate.

Thomas H. Miller, a Manuscript Specialist with the SHS, interviewed Lowell McMurtrey on August 20, 2004 (4 days before his 82nd birthday), at the Willow Care Nursing Home as part of SHC's Ex-POW Oral History Program. Coincidentally, 4 months later, I would visit Mr. McMurtrey at Willow Care.

At the time of the SHS interview, Mr. McMurtrey suffered from age-related memory issues, but with skillful questioning by Mr. Miller and gentle prompts from his wife Margaret, he provided lucid, factual information,

During the interview, both Lowell and Margaret confirmed that he was drafted. When asked by Miller if he wanted to go to war, he responded, "No, I didn't want to go to war. They drafted me."

The regulations of the Selective Service Act of 1940 allowed deferments that included farm workers, the medical community, the ministry, and when dependents required support of the registrant, but not for being married. According to Cengage Encyclopedia.Com, "Volunteering was prohibited in late 1942, and the draft became the only way to enter the armed forces . . . a majority of the men donned the uniform via the draft." Before the prohibition, one could volunteer and choose the desired branch of service.

While in Africa as part of the 7th Army, he was assigned to guard General Patton's tent one night. I can only imagine the awe a boy from Willow Springs felt meeting the notorious general. In the SHS interview, Miller asked him if he had any interaction with General Patton. Mr. McMurtrey responded,

"Yeah, he says, 'Go get me something to drink. I'm out of water.' So I went and got him some water. He said over there somebody had some water. I came back and it fell in the ditch. I had to go fill it up again . . .. I got back with the water, and he said, 'Thank you, soldier.'"

Private Lowell McMurtrey in Italy in 1944. *Courtesy of State Historical Society of Missouri from the Lowell and Margaret M. McMurtrey Papers 1942-1971 (C4172).*

Margaret added to the story. "But the funny part was you see, he told him to go get some water, and he said you weren't supposed to . . . if you are guarding somebody . . . you weren't supposed to leave them."

After the African campaign, he transferred to the 5th Army commanded by General Mark Wayne Clark. The *Willow Springs News* reported: "After being stationed in North Africa a short time, he participated in the invasion of Sicily and later in the invasion of Italy. He has been in action since he went overseas in May of last year."

The West Plains *Journal-Gazette* reported: "Young McMurtrey has been in the battle areas since May 10 of this year when he arrived in North Africa with replacement troops, which were immediately sent to the front. He participated in the Battle of Sicily and helped make the landing on Salerno beach [Italy]. Although his letters gave no details of his experience, they had revealed to his parents he has been through close brushes with death."

So, imagine the terror on March 2, 1944, when Lowell's mother, Mrs. Adel McMurtrey, received the following Western Union telegram from the Adjutant General of the Army: "The Secretary of War desires me to express his deep regret that your son Private First Class Lowell M. McMurtrey has been reported missing in action since three February in Italy. [As] Further details or other information are received you will be promptly notified." And imagine having to break the news to her daughter-in-law Margaret.

The same day, the *Journal-Gazette* reported that Judge M.K. McMurtrey and Mrs. McMurtrey were with their son's "grief-stricken wife, the former Miss Margaret Mitchell, daughter of Justice Roy Mitchell and Mrs. Mitchell."

In case you are wondering (I was), why was the telegram sent to his mother and not his wife? Although Margaret received subsequent correspondence from the War Department, the information saved in the SHC files, and the newspaper accounts also show, some initial notifications went to his mother. I'm not sure of the protocol at the time, but, for whatever reason, I suspect the Casualty Notification Card that service members complete, may have listed his mother.

Western Union telegram from the Secretary of War sent March 1, 1944, to Lowell McMurtrey's mother advising that her son was missing in action. *Courtesy of State Historical Society of Missouri from the Lowell and Margaret M. McMurtrey Papers 1942-1971 (C4172).*

On April 29, 1944, Adel McMurtrey received a letter from Brigadier Robert H. Dunlap in Washington, DC. "Up to the present time no further information has reached the War Department regarding your son's whereabouts. A report has been received, however, which states that Private McMurtrey was a crew member of a tank assigned the mission of attacking the enemy in the north end of Cassino, Italy, in conjunction with an infantry attack. No trace was found of your son or his tank after the enemy was engaged."

Imagine the thoughts that raced through her mind when she read, "No trace was found." Was he blown up? Local newspapers reported the family feared he was no longer alive.

Over four months passed, waiting and worrying, before the family heard anything. Finally, on June 7, 1944, Margaret received a telegram from the War Department: "[The] Following unofficial short wave broadcast from Germany has been inter-cepted Quote I am a prisoner of the Germans. I am treated well will write later I love you Darling Lowell McMurtrey. Unquote. Pending further confirmation this report does not establish his status to be a prisoner of war stop. Any additional information received will be furnished stop."

The *Howell County Gazette* reporting on this news implied the broadcast was authentic. "The phrase 'I love you, darling' was one which Lowell used in talking to Mrs. McMurtrey. Also there was no other way of anyone knowing the box number and address of Mrs. McMurtrey at Willow Springs."

Lowell McMurtrey—Part 3

ON JUNE 7, 1944, after hearing nothing about her husband for over four months, Lowell McMurtrey's wife Margaret received a telegram from the War Department stating a shortwave broadcast from Germany had been intercepted, in which Lowell was purportedly heard saying he was a prisoner of war. Several days later, his mother Adel McMurtrey received a telegram from the War Department: "Your son Private First Class Lowell McMurtrey is a prisoner of war of the German government."

One of the things I learned researching this article was people in the United States listened to overseas broadcasts on shortwave radios for war news. If they picked up information about an individual service member, they would mail postcards and letters to family members across the country. The McMurtrey files in Missouri State Historical (SHS) records contain numerous such cards and letters.

The *Howell County Gazette* reported Margaret McMurtrey ". . . received over thirty letters and telegrams from people, mostly from the east, who had also heard the broadcast. One of these letters described the voice as American and deep and slow which is the way Lowell talks."

Lowell was captured February 24, 1944, at the battle of Casino, Italy, after his tank became disabled and was surrounded by enemy soldiers. The West Plains *Journal-Gazette* reported that "he was shot through the chest at that time." However, Lowell's statement in the interview conducted by Manuscript Specialist Tom Miller, as part of the SHS Oral History Program, Collection C3975, on August 20, 2004, differs from the newspaper account. Apparently, a shell fragment hit him in the chest severely damaging his lung after German soldiers herded Lowell and other prisoners into a barn.

From the SHS 2004 interview:

Miller: "Were you ever wounded?"

McMurtrey: "Yeah, I got wounded in the lung. A shell came through this barn, hit me in the lung. I fell on the floor."

Miller: "And that came through a barn, you said:"

McMurtrey: "Came through the top of the barn."

■　■　■　■

Miller: "Oh, this was after you'd been taken prisoner:"

McMurtrey: "After I was taken prisoner."

Miller: "Then you were wounded. I see. And this was American fire that was coming in."

McMurtrey: "American fire."

Miller: So, you were hit by friendly fire."

McMurtrey: "Friendly fire."

German doctors treated Lowell for two months at a hospital

in Italy, where, the *Journal-Gazette* reported Lowell saying, "he got the best of medical treatment." From the hospital, Germans soldiers loaded Lowell and other prisoners onto a train car and shipped them to a Stalag in Germany. From there he was transferred by railway to Stalag II B at Hammerstein in northern Germany.

During his confinement as a POW, he was able to send and receive mail with restrictions as to size and content, namely, postcards. The cards he sent had postage stamps with Adolf Hitler's portrait.

An interesting letter in the SHS files, dated March 10, 1945, came from teachers at WSHS saying, "We want to let you know that we are thinking of you often . . . ." Several teachers signed it, including, T.G. Munford, Jessie Munford, Lorene Masnor, and Myrtle Dunivin—teachers Lowell had in school, and with whom he would later be a teaching colleague. [Many HCN readers, including me, had those same teachers.]

Lowell's correspondence reflected he was generally treated well by the guards, but the food was bad. The *Journal-Gazette* reported, "They would have starved without their Red Cross Packages. For breakfast they had a cup of coffee, for dinner a pint of grass soup, which was almost always wormy and which was made out of dandelions, and for supper about three slices of bread."

In the SHS interview, Margaret and Lowell said they wrote each other every day. When asked by the interviewer how it made him feel when he received Margaret's letters, he said, "Real good. I didn't know she still loved me."

As bad as circumstances were, they were about to get worse. As the Russians advanced from the East, the Germans feared Stalag II B would be overtaken and the prisoners liberated. On January 29, 1945, the guards began marching the prisoners on a 600-mile slog toward Munich during the cold, northern German winter. Lowell said the snow was over his boots and they slept outdoors or in barns and got lice. They only had rations for the first week and then had to live off the land.

The *Journal-Gazette* posted, "He was one of the twelve hundred that started the march from the Stalag. They marched 600 miles in two months and only four hundred and fifty-eight survived."

The survivors of the forced march ended up at Stalag VII A, a large POW camp at the outskirts of Moosburg, Germany, about 25 miles from Munich. After 16 months as a prisoner of war, this is where his captivity ended. In a letter to his parents, reprinted in the Victory Edition of the *Journal-Gazette*, Lowell said, "The Russians liberated me on April 29 [1945]."

Other newspapers also indicated the Russians had liberated him, which suggests a different picture of the circumstances of his release than the actual facts. Of the Russians, Margaret stated in the SHS interview, "[T]hey didn't liberate you because you took off before they got there. Lowell responded, "Took off before they got there . . . we knew the Americans were nearby."

With the Russians approaching, German guards began deserting the Stalag. Although Lowell said that he had never tried to escape, when the German guards evacuated from Stalag VII A, he and fellow prisoner Darrell Hibbard walked to the American forces. In the letter to his parents, reprinted in the West Plains Journal, Lowell wrote, "They [Russians] treated us very nice, got plenty of rides to the American lines." The *Journal-Gazette* reported Lowell said he "kissed the first American soldier he saw after getting loose."

Margaret and Lowell McMurtrey in Hot Springs, Arkansas, September 1945. *Courtesy of State Historical Society of Missouri from the Lowell and Margaret M. McMurtrey Papers 1942-1971 (C4172).*

Lowell departed for America from LaHarve, France, on a naval transport and arrived home on June 28, 1945. He received an extended furlough and arrived by train at Cabool where Troop G Highway Patrolman Ted R. Taylor picked him up and drove him to Willow Springs.

In September 1945, Lowell and Margaret traveled to Hot Springs, Arkansas, for two weeks of rest and recouperation. Lowell continued to have physical pain from his wound that required an operation at the Veteran's Hospital in Memphis, Tennessee, in February 1946.

Lowell's official date of separation from the Army was October 13, 1945. His Separation Qualification Record shows he was awarded four battle stars and a Good Conduct Medal.

For those who didn't know Lowell McMurtrey, now, you do. For those who did, I hope you know him better—I do.

My thanks to the State Historical Society of Missouri for the information obtained from the Lowell and Margaret M. McMurtrey Papers (C4172), 1942–1971.

Remembering a Special Veteran

WITH VETERANS DAY APPROACHING, I am remembering another World War II service member, George C. Anstey, M.D.— my father-in-law. He served as Battalion Surgeon in the 3rd Armored Division at the Battle of the Bulge.

George Anstey, born in 1917, grew up in Messina, Iowa, with his father, a veterinarian/farmer, his mother, and three older sisters. Life during the Great Depression came with the usual hardships and a few more for him. One night George witnessed a flaming cross erected on their front yard by the Ku Klux Klan. His family was Catholic.

At the age of five, a farm accident left him paralyzed from the waist down. George's father had set him astraddle a horse that was pulling a wagon loaded with corn sileage. The horse reared and fell backwards pinning George underneath. For several months George had to be lifted in and out of bed and could only get around by pulling himself about in a child's wagon. With exercises and a brace his father devised, George regained the ability to walk. In later life, the injury caused pain, but did not prevent him from becoming an ardent and accomplished golfer.

After undergraduate school at Creighton University in Omaha, Nebraska, he received his M.D. degree from Creighton Medical School. During medical school, he met his future wife Catherine and took her to a football game on their first date. After graduation in 1942, they married on February 27, 1943. Uncle Sam, with a draft notice in hand, waited in the vestibule.

After training at the Medical Field Service School in Carlisle, Pennsylvania, from July 5— August 12, 1943, he became part of General Omar Bradley's First Army in the European Theater, as battalion surgeon in the 3rd Armored Division commanded by Major General Maurice Rose.

Dr. George C. Anstey as an Army captain in World War II.

For readers unfamiliar with military unit organization, a field army, which may have 50,000 soldiers, is commanded by a 4-star general and is subdivided into corps, divisions, regiments, battalions, companies, platoons, and squads. A major general (2-star) commands a division, which can have 3 or more battalions. A battalion can have 300–1,000 men, with several companies.

A medical battalion, much smaller, is an organic part of the division, and is commanded by the battalion surgeon.

The personnel consisted of the battalion surgeon (a captain), assistant surgeon, medical technicians, frontline medics, litter bearers, and drivers.

A battalion aid station, unlike a MASH unit as depicted in the TV series, provided the forwardmost medical treatment for frontline troops and could be as close as a quarter mile away in a tent or abandoned house. It isn't surprising the Army awarded George the Combat Medical Badge for performing medical duties while being engaged by the enemy.

A battalion surgeon was not a rear-echelon position, particularly with a commanding general like Maurice Rose, who was known for his aggressive leadership style, giving personal orders to his commanders at the forward edge of the battle area.

A captured German semi-automatic pistol "issued" to Captain Anstey.

By spring 1945, the 3rd Armored Division had spearheaded the First Army's charge through Belgium and was the first unit to reach Germany. On March 30, 1945, General Rose rode in a jeep behind a tank at the front of a small convoy south of Paderborn, Germany, where they encountered gunfire and the lead tank was hit and destroyed.

Although newspaper accounts vary, evasive action failed and they were surrounded by German tanks. A German soldier emerged from a tank hatch barking commands that General Rose didn't understand. As he unholstered his pistol to surrender, the German opened fire with a machine gun killing him.

George rode in an armored car directly behind General Rose's jeep. Under the Geneva Convention rules, medical personnel as non-combatants were not issued firearms, and accordingly, were not legitimate targets. But when they were surrounded by German soldiers, an officer handed George a pistol and said, "They're going to kill us all."

Based on statements by General Rose's aid, Major Robert Bellinger, the Carroll, Iowa, *Times Herald* reported "Bellinger and other officers and men in the armored car made a dash for freedom and escaped, making their way to headquarters hours later."

In addition to the Combat Medical Badge, George received a Bronze Star and the European Theater Campaign Medal, with a battle star. Of the Bronze Star, an Iowa newspaper reported in 1945, "Captain Anstey . . . braved heavy enemy artillery, mortar, small arms and automatic weapon fire to care for and evacuate the wounded."

George returned home to Catherine and a baby son and began an OB–GYN residency in St. Louis. Over the course of fifty years, he and Catherine raised four sons and one daughter, and

Dr. Anstey maintained a successful medical practice delivering babies numbering in thousands. In 1970, he was elected president and chief of the Missouri Baptist Hospital medical staff. In 1975, he was certified as a fellow of the American College of Obstetricians and Gynecologists.

But late in his retirement, Alzheimer's disease dealt him a hard blow. Alzheimer's disease, like a soul-sucking dementor in the Harry Potter books, robbed him of a brilliant mind, leaving him without the personal dignity of dressing or bathing himself.

Alzheimer's is a thief, but not a back-alley stick-up artist operating in the shadows. It's an embezzler—taking only a little at first—but cold and patient as it accumulates rogue proteins to form Beta-amyloid plaque in the brain.

When he couldn't remember the combination to his locker at the golf club, it became difficult to discount other symptoms as mere age-related memory loss. He had used the same simple combination—0-0-0—for twenty years.

He began repeating an incident from his childhood, over and over. "You know, a horse fell on me and left me paralyzed for the summer . . . ."

As the disease progressed, relatives became unrecognizable to him. At a birthday party for his great grandson, he nudged me and nodded toward his oldest son. "See that bird over there—I think we're related to him." Perverse humor became a defense mechanism as family members repeated the story and laughed.

Humor also helped when embarrassing occurrences tried the patience of family caregivers. One day when Catherine was upstairs, George answered a phone call from a life-long friend. George told her there were rough-looking strangers in the house playing cards. Believing the fantasy to be true, the friend called the police, who showed up at the house, to the surprise and embarrassment of Catherine. It was as if he had become Elwood P. Dowd from the movie *Harvey*.

Occasionally technology produced lucid intervals that we clung to as signs of improvement. Using Google Earth on a laptop, I zoomed to the main street of his hometown. The images jump-started him to reality. He spoke with clarity of the businesses that had occupied the buildings, and the location of his home and neighbors. And on short road trips, with the car radio tuned to a 1940s station, he would smile and sing along with Bing Crosby or the Dorsey brothers. But these were short-lived miracles.

Eventually, most of his conversations replayed scenes from days past, with imaginary relatives. He often mistook his wife for his sister, who had died years before.

Still, from the legacy of his well-lived life, blessings occurred. Of the thousands of babies Dr. Anstey delivered, one became a priest, who, fittingly, presided at his funeral. To an overflow audience, Father Brown proclaimed, "Dr. Anstey delivered me into to this world, and now I get to deliver him into the next."

In the end we triumph, understanding that the memory stolen by the disease can't erase the memories he left behind. I never met a more honorable man.

About the Author

LONNIE WHITAKER ATTENDED A two-room school in the Missouri Ozarks and later earned a Juris Doctor degree from the University of Missouri School of Law. He served as a Special Assistant U.S. Attorney and retired as district counsel for a federal agency and now works as a writer. His novels, *Geese to a Poor Market* and *Soda Fountain Blues*, both won the Ozark Writers' League Best Book of the Year Award. He is the author of an award-winning children's book series about Mulligan the cat. His short stories have been published by Chicken Soup for the Soul, Five Star Publishing, *Missouri Life*, *The Ozark Mountaineer*, and several anthologies. His newspaper column, "The Way We Were . . . Personal Reflections on Life in the Ozarks" is published bi-weekly by the *Howell County News*, and has won multiple awards from the Missouri Writers Guild. He and his wife live in Missouri with two dogs and a rescued tomcat.

Dear Reader

THANK YOU SO MUCH for reading *The Way We Were . . . Personal Reflections on Life in the Ozarks*, and allowing me to share my observations about growing up in the Missouri Ozarks in the 1950 and 60s. I hope my literary efforts provided a smile or two, and, perhaps, took you down your own personal memory lane.

Please take a moment to post a review on Amazon, Facebook, or other reviewing site. Positive reviews make a tremendous difference in the success of a book, and I will be most grateful.

I am available to speak at your organization or book club, in person, or online. Contact me at www.lonniewhitaker.com.

—LONNIE WHITAKER